# 150 Recipes
## in a
# 13x9 Pan

## Gooseberry Patch

An imprint of Globe Pequot
246 Goose Lane
Guilford, CT 06437

# www.gooseberrypatch.com

## 1•800•854•6673

Copyright 2016, Gooseberry Patch  978-1-62093-230-8

## Do you have a tried & true recipe...

tip, craft or memory that you'd like to see featured in
a **Gooseberry Patch** cookbook? Visit our website at
**www.gooseberrypatch.com** and follow the
easy steps to submit your favorite family recipe.
Or send them to us at:

Gooseberry Patch
PO Box 812
Columbus, OH 43216-0812

Don't forget to include the number of servings your recipe makes,
plus your name, address, phone number and email address. If we
select your recipe, your name will appear right along with it...
and you'll receive a **FREE** copy of the book!

# Contents

# Dedication

To cooks everywhere who know that a steamy
hot casserole or a warm bubbly dessert can
warm the heart as well as fill the tummy.

# Breakfasts to Wake Up For

## Sausage & Red Pepper Strata

*A delicious layered casserole to make the night before...
in the morning, just pop it in the oven!*

1 lb. ground pork sausage
1 t. dried oregano
1/2 t. red pepper flakes
8 slices French bread, cubed
1 red pepper, diced
2 t. dried parsley

8 eggs, beaten
2 c. evaporated milk
2 t. Dijon mustard
1/2 t. pepper
1 c. shredded sharp Cheddar cheese

Brown sausage with oregano and red pepper flakes in a skillet over medium heat; drain and set aside. Arrange bread cubes in the bottom of a greased 13"x9" baking pan; top with sausage mixture, red pepper and parsley. Set aside. In a large bowl, whisk together eggs, milk, mustard and pepper; pour evenly over sausage mixture. Cover tightly with aluminum foil and refrigerate 8 hours to overnight. Bake, covered, at 350 degrees for 55 minutes. Remove foil; sprinkle with cheese and bake for an additional 5 minutes, or until cheese is melted. Serves 4 to 6.

## Easy Egg Bake

*Need a quick breakfast to share with friends? This just takes a few minutes to put together.*

20-oz. pkg. refrigerated diced
   potatoes with onions
6-oz. pkg. precooked bacon
6 to 8 eggs, beaten

1/4 c. milk
salt and pepper to taste
8-oz. pkg. shredded sharp Cheddar
   cheese

Spray a 13"x9" baking pan with non-stick vegetable spray. Spread potatoes in pan. Using kitchen scissors, snip bacon into pieces over potatoes. Bake, uncovered, at 350 degrees for about 15 minutes; remove from oven. Whisk together eggs and milk; pour over baked layer. Sprinkle with salt, pepper and cheese. Return to oven, uncovered, for 25 to 30 minutes, until eggs are set and cheese is melted. Cut into squares. Serves 8.

Sausage & Red Pepper Strata

Crescent Breakfast Casserole

## Crescent Breakfast Casserole

*Quick & easy for a chilly morning...it makes a hearty, filling supper too.*

8-oz. tube refrigerated crescent
   rolls
6 to 8 eggs, beaten
1/4 c. milk
3/4 c. finely shredded Cheddar
   cheese

1/2 c. bacon, crisply cooked, or
   ground pork sausage, browned
   and crumbled
salt and pepper to taste

Line the bottom and sides of a lightly greased 13"x9" baking pan with unrolled crescents. Pinch seams together to seal; set aside. In a bowl, stir together remaining ingredients. Pour egg mixture over crescents in baking pan. Bake, uncovered, at 350 degrees for about 20 minutes, until golden and center is set. Serves 8.

9

Make school-day breakfasts fun! Along with Crescent Breakfast Casserole, serve milk with twisty straws.

## Baked Apple Pancake

*Mmm...tender apples, brown sugar and cinnamon!*

4 apples, peeled, cored and sliced
1/2 c. butter, softened and divided
1/2 c. brown sugar, packed
1 t. cinnamon

6 eggs, beaten
1 c. all-purpose flour
1 c. milk
3 T. sugar

Combine apples, 1/4 cup butter, brown sugar and cinnamon in a microwave-safe bowl. Microwave on high setting about 2 to 4 minutes, until tender. Stir; spoon into a lightly greased 13"x9" baking pan and set aside. In a separate bowl, combine remaining ingredients; whisk until smooth and spread over apple mixture. Bake, uncovered, at 425 degrees for 25 minutes. Cut into squares; serve warm. Serves 6 to 8.

Make fancy bacon curls to garnish breakfast plates. Fry bacon until browned but not crisp. Immediately roll up slices and fasten each with a toothpick. Drain on paper towels. Mmm!

Baked Apple Pancake

Crustless Ham & Spinach Quiche

## Crustless Ham & Spinach Quiche

*This satisfying egg dish is terrific for breakfast, lunch or dinner.*
*It's good either warm or cold, travels well and freezes nicely.*
*What more could you want?*

1 doz. eggs
2 c. whipping cream or milk
1/2 t. garlic powder
1/2 t. dried oregano
1/8 t. pepper

1 c. cooked ham, finely diced
10-oz. pkg. frozen spinach, thawed
  and drained
1/4 to 1/2 c. onion, finely diced
2 c. shredded Cheddar cheese

In a large bowl, combine eggs and cream or milk. Beat well with an electric mixer on low speed. Stir in seasonings; set aside. Sprinkle remaining ingredients evenly into a lightly greased 13"x9" baking pan. Slowly pour egg mixture into pan. Bake, uncovered, at 350 degrees for 45 to 50 minutes, until golden and a knife tip inserted in center tests clean. Allow to cool slightly before cutting into squares. Makes 8 servings.

A juicy fruit salad is perfect with a savory quiche. Cut up an assortment of melons, berries and other fresh fruit...toss with your favorite poppy seed dressing.

## Tex-Mex Egg Puff

*Mix, bake and serve...how easy is that? Serve with your favorite salsa.*

1 doz. eggs, beaten
1/2 c. butter, melted and cooled
　slightly
1/2 c. all-purpose flour
1 t. baking powder
1/2 t. salt

2 4-oz. cans chopped green chiles,
　drained
16-oz. pkg. shredded Monterey
　Jack cheese
16-oz. container small-curd cottage
　cheese

In a large bowl, combine all ingredients except chiles and cheeses; whisk until smooth. Fold in chiles, shredded cheese and cottage cheese; spoon into a greased 13"x9" baking pan. Bake, uncovered, at 350 degrees for 35 to 40 minutes, until set. Cut into squares. Serves 8 to 10.

## Bubble Breakfast Pizza

*A quick, delicious breakfast that's sure to be a hit! Try it with crisp bacon instead of sausage too.*

16-oz. pkg. ground pork sausage
1 doz. eggs
1/2 c. milk
1 T. butter

16-oz. tube refrigerated jumbo
　biscuits
8-oz. pkg. pasteurized process
　cheese spread, sliced

Brown sausage in a large skillet over medium heat; drain and set aside. Whisk together eggs and milk in a large bowl. Wipe out skillet; melt butter over low heat and add egg mixture. Cook and stir until eggs are lightly scrambled. While eggs are cooking, separate biscuits and press into a greased 13"x9" baking pan, forming a crust. Spoon scrambled eggs over biscuits; top with sausage and cheese. Bake, uncovered, at 375 degrees for 30 minutes, or until biscuits are set and cheese melts. Makes 8 servings.

A pizza cutter makes quick work of dividing up servings
right in the baking pan.

Tex-Mex Egg Puff

Orange-Cinnamon French Toast

## Orange-Cinnamon French Toast

*Add a teaspoon of orange zest for even more citrusy flavor.*

2 to 4 T. butter, melted
2 T. honey
1/2 t. cinnamon
3 eggs, beaten

1/2 c. frozen orange juice
   concentrate, partially thawed
1/8 t. salt
6 slices French bread

Combine butter, honey and cinnamon in a 13"x9" baking pan and set aside. In a shallow bowl, whisk together eggs, orange juice and salt. Dip bread slices into egg mixture, coating both sides. Arrange dipped bread slices in baking pan. Bake, uncovered, at 400 degrees for 15 to 20 minutes, until golden. Serves 3 to 4.

Freshly grated orange zest adds so much flavor to recipes and it's easy to keep on hand. Whenever you use an orange, just grate the peel first. Keep it frozen in an airtight container up to 2 months.

## Blueberry French Toast

*A new and yummy twist on French toast for the whole family to enjoy.*

2 c. fresh or frozen blueberries
2 T. cornstarch
1/4 c. sugar
1/2 c. orange juice
1/2 c. plus 3 T. water, divided

3 eggs, beaten
6 slices bread
2 T. butter, melted
cinnamon-sugar to taste

Spread blueberries in a greased 13"x9" baking pan; set aside. In a bowl, combine cornstarch, sugar, orange juice and 1/2 cup water; pour over blueberries. In a shallow bowl, whisk together eggs and remaining water. Dip bread slices into egg mixture; arrange over blueberries in pan. Brush bread slices with butter and sprinkle with cinnamon-sugar. Bake, uncovered, at 350 degrees for 15 to 20 minutes, until bread is lightly toasted and sauce is bubbly and thickened. Serve toast slices topped with blueberry mixture from pan. Serves 6.

Day-old bread is excellent for making French toast and breakfast stratas. It keeps its texture better than very fresh bread...it's thrifty too!

Blueberry French Toast

Caramel Rolls

## Caramel Rolls

*Only the freshest butter will do for Grandma's homemade caramel rolls!*

1 c. brown sugar, packed
1 c. whipping cream
3-1/2 c. all-purpose flour, divided
3/4 c. sugar, divided
1 env. active dry yeast
1 t. salt

1 c. water
1/2 c. plus 2 T. butter, softened
  and divided
1 egg, beaten
2 t. cinnamon

Stir together brown sugar and cream in an ungreased 13"x9" baking pan; set aside. In a large bowl, blend 1-1/2 cups flour, 1/4 cup sugar, yeast and salt. In a saucepan over medium heat, heat water and 2 tablespoons butter until very warm, about 110 to 115 degrees. Add warm liquid and egg to flour mixture. Beat with an electric mixer on low speed until moistened; beat at medium speed for 3 minutes. Stir in remaining flour. Knead dough for 2 to 3 minutes on a floured surface. Roll out on a floured surface to a 15-inch by 7-inch rectangle. Combine remaining sugar, remaining butter and cinnamon; spread over dough. Starting on one long edge, roll up tightly. Seal edges; slice into 15 rolls. Place rolls, cut-side down, in prepared pan. Cover with a tea towel and let rise in a warm place until double in size, 35 to 45 minutes. Bake, uncovered, at 400 degrees for 20 to 25 minutes, until golden. Makes 15 rolls.

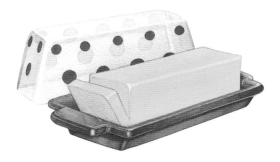

Store brown sugar in an airtight container to keep it soft. Too late?
For a quick fix, place hardened brown sugar in a microwave-safe bowl
and cover first with a damp paper towel, then plastic wrap. Microwave
on high for 30 seconds to one minute, fluff with a fork and
use immediately.

## Cherry Streusel Coffee Cake

*You'll be proud to serve this easy-to-assemble coffee cake...it's irresistible!*

18-1/2 oz. pkg. yellow cake mix, divided
1 c. all-purpose flour
1 env. active dry yeast
2 eggs, beaten
2/3 c. warm water
5 T. butter, melted
21-oz. can cherry pie filling
2 T. sugar
Garnish: chopped nuts

In a large bowl, combine 1-1/2 cups dry cake mix, flour, yeast, eggs and warm water. Stir for 2 minutes. Spread batter in a greased 13"x9" baking pan. In a separate bowl, blend melted butter and remaining cake mix; set aside. Spoon pie filling over batter in pan. Crumble butter mixture over pie filling. Sprinkle sugar over top. Bake, uncovered, at 375 degrees for 30 minutes; cool. Drizzle with glaze; sprinkle nuts on top. Serves 15.

### Glaze:
1 c. powdered sugar
1 T. corn syrup
1 to 2 T. water

Combine powdered sugar and corn syrup. Stir in enough water to form a glaze consistency.

## Lemon-Blueberry Coffee Cake

*A tried & true favorite...the combination of the lemon and blueberry is oh-so good! Delicious warm or cold.*

18-1/4 oz. pkg. lemon cake mix
1/2 c. butter, softened
2 eggs
2/3 c. milk
1 c. fresh or frozen blueberries

In a large bowl, combine dry cake mix and butter; mix until crumbly. Set aside 1-1/4 cups of crumb mixture for topping. To remaining crumb mixture, add eggs and milk. Beat with an electric mixer on medium speed for 2 minutes. Spread batter in a greased and floured 13"x9" baking pan. Top with fresh or frozen berries and reserved crumb mixture. Bake at 325 degrees for 25 to 30 minutes. Makes 10 to 12 servings.

Cherry Streusel Coffee Cake

Make-Ahead Cheese & Egg Casserole

## Make-Ahead Cheese & Egg Casserole

*This cheesy casserole is great for weekend breakfasts or a special brunch.*

3 c. seasoned croutons
15 eggs, beaten
2 c. milk
1 t. seasoned salt

1 t. pepper
3/4 t. onion powder
2 T. fresh chives, chopped
1-1/2 c. shredded Cheddar cheese

Place croutons in a 13"x9" baking pan coated with non-stick vegetable spray; set aside. In a bowl, whisk together eggs, milk and seasonings; stir in cheese. Pour over croutons. Cover and refrigerate for 8 hours to overnight, stirring once. Uncover and stir. Bake, uncovered, at 350 degrees for 30 minutes, or until eggs are set. Serves 8 to 10.

Looking ahead to a busy day tomorrow? Get your family's day off to a great start with an overnight breakfast dish that can be assembled the night before and baked in the morning.

# Breakfasts to Wake Up For

## Sweet & Spicy Bacon

*Try this delectable bacon at your next brunch...guests will love it!*

1/2 c. brown sugar, packed
2 T. chili powder
1 t. ground cumin
1 t. cumin seed

1 t. ground coriander
1/4 t. cayenne pepper
10 thick slices bacon

Line a shallow 13"x9" baking pan with aluminum foil. Place a wire rack in pan and set aside. In a small bowl, combine all ingredients except bacon; sprinkle mixture onto a large piece of wax paper. Press bacon slices into mixture, turning to coat well. Arrange slices in a single layer in prepared pan; place pan on center rack of oven. Bake at 400 degrees for 12 minutes; turn slices over. Bake for an additional 10 minutes, or until deeply golden. Drain on paper towels; serve warm. Serves 4 to 5.

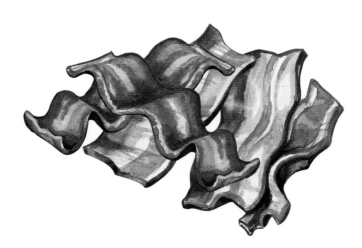

On a sunny day, take brunch outdoors! Spread out a quilt on the picnic table, gather everyone 'round and enjoy the warm weather.

Sweet & Spicy Bacon

Block's Pimento & Cheese Grits Casserole

## Brock's Pimento & Cheese Grits Casserole

*Spoon sautéed shrimp over top for a really special down-south treat!*

3 c. quick-cooking grits, uncooked
1/2 c. butter
1/2 c. whipping cream
1 t. salt
16-oz. pkg. shredded Cheddar cheese

4-oz. jar diced pimentos, drained
1 c. mayonnaise
8-oz. pkg. cream cheese, softened
2 t. pepper
1/2 c. green onions, chopped

Cook grits according to package directions. Transfer grits to a large bowl; stir in butter, cream and salt. In a separate bowl, combine remaining ingredients except onions; mix well. Add cheese mixture to grits mixture; stir together. Pour into a greased 13"x9" baking pan. Bake, uncovered, at 375 degrees for 35 to 40 minutes, until bubbly. Top with onions. Serves 8.

Planning a midday brunch? Along with breakfast foods like baked eggs, coffee cake and cereal, offer a light, savory main dish or 2 for those who have already enjoyed breakfast.

Butterscotch Granola

## Butterscotch Granola

*The best granola you'll ever taste! Sprinkle it over berry yogurt
for a wonderful breakfast treat.*

10 c. long-cooking oats, uncooked
2 sleeves graham crackers, crushed
2 c. sweetened flaked coconut
1 c. pecans, finely chopped
3/4 c. brown sugar, packed

1 t. baking soda
1 t. salt
2 c. butter, melted
16-oz. pkg. butterscotch chips

Mix together all ingredients except butterscotch chips in a greased deep
13"x9" baking pan. Bake, uncovered, at 300 degrees for 40 minutes,
stirring every 10 minutes. Add butterscotch chips during the last 5 minutes;
mix well after melted to distribute evenly. Cool; store in an airtight
container. Makes 5 quarts.

## Applesauce Baked Oatmeal

*Add more applesauce and less sugar as you wish, to suit your own taste.*

1-1/2 c. quick-cooking oats,
  uncooked
1/4 c. sugar
1 t. baking powder
3/4 t. salt
1/2 c. milk

1/4 c. butter, softened
1 egg, beaten
1/4 c. applesauce
1 t. vanilla extract
Garnish: warm milk, brown sugar,
  sliced fruit

Combine oats, sugar, baking powder and salt; mix well. Add remaining
ingredients except garnish; mix to a smooth, thin consistency. Spread
evenly in a greased 13"x9" baking pan. Bake, uncovered, at 350 degrees
for 25 to 30 minutes, until edges turn golden. Serve immediately, stirring in
additional warm milk as needed. Top with brown sugar or sliced fruit, as
desired. Makes 6 to 8 servings.

A fresh breakfast side dish...fruit kabobs! Just slide pineapple chunks,
apple slices, orange wedges and strawberries onto a wooden skewer.
They can even be slipped into breakfast smoothies or frosty juices.

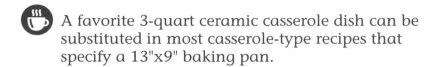

A favorite 3-quart ceramic casserole dish can be substituted in most casserole-type recipes that specify a 13"x9" baking pan.

Are family members on different morning schedules? Divide the ingredients for a breakfast casserole among individual custard cups or ramekins and bake as needed.

Pancakes in a jiffy...no standing over the stove! Mix up batter and pour it into a well buttered 13"x9" baking pan. Bake at 350 degrees for 20 to 24 minutes, until pancake tests done with a toothpick. Cut into squares and serve.

Ovens can vary, so set a kitchen timer when the pan goes into the oven. Check for doneness after the shortest baking time given...if a little more time is needed, be sure to watch carefully.

# Square Meals

## Spicy Rubbed Pork Tenderloin

*A great go-to recipe for company or a busy day at home. Serve with roasted new potatoes.*

1 to 3 T. chili powder, to taste
1 t. salt
1 t. pepper
1/4 t. ground ginger
1/4 t. dried thyme
1/4 t. dry mustard
1 lb. pork tenderloin fillet

Mix all spices together in a bowl. Rub desired amount of spice mixture over both sides of tenderloin. Wrap tightly in aluminum foil; refrigerate for 8 hours to overnight. Place foil package in a shallow 13"x9" baking pan. Bake at 350 degrees for one hour. Remove tenderloin to a platter; let stand for 10 minutes. Slice and serve with natural juices. Makes 8 servings.

Baked apples are a scrumptious treat and go especially well with pork. Core apples nearly through and place in a greased baking pan. Fill each apple with a teaspoon of honey, a teaspoon of butter and a little cinnamon. Bake at 350 degrees for 35 to 45 minutes, until tender. Serve warm.

Spicy Rubbed Pork Tenderloin

Patsy's Stuffed Pork Chops

# Square Meals

## Patsy's Stuffed Pork Chops

*Prepare for raves and recipe requests whenever you serve these tasty chops!*

2 6-oz. pkgs. pork or savory herb
   stuffing mix
8 boneless pork chops
2 T. oil

3 cloves garlic, sliced
salt and pepper to taste
2 c. applesauce
cinnamon to taste

Prepare stuffing mix according to package instructions; set aside. Cut a pocket into the center of each pork chop, slicing horizontally into the side. Evenly stuff chops with prepared stuffing. Drizzle oil in a 13"x9" baking pan; sprinkle with garlic. Arrange chops in pan and season with salt and pepper. Top each chop with 1/4 cup applesauce and sprinkle with cinnamon. Bake, uncovered, at 425 degrees for 30 minutes, or until chops are no longer pink. Makes 8 servings.

## Meatball-Stuffed Shells

*A super-easy recipe that's great for a quick dinner... just add a tossed salad.*

12-oz. pkg. jumbo pasta shells,
   uncooked
28-oz. jar pasta sauce, divided

36 frozen Italian meatballs, thawed
2 c. shredded mozzarella cheese

Cook pasta according to package directions; drain and rinse in cold water. Spread 1/2 cup pasta sauce in a greased 13"x9" baking pan. Tuck a meatball into each shell; arrange shells in pan. Top with remaining sauce; add cheese. Cover; bake at 350 degrees for 35 minutes. Uncover and bake 10 more minutes. Serves 6 to 8.

Keep a can of non-stick vegetable spray on hand to quickly spritz on a baking pan for easy clean-up later.

## Baked Chicken Jambalaya

*Looking for a flavorful new dinner recipe? The whole family will love this one!*

1 lb. smoked beef sausage, sliced
1/4 c. butter
4 c. cooked chicken, cubed
16-oz. pkg. frozen mixed
   vegetables, thawed
1 onion, sliced

4 stalks celery, sliced
1 green pepper, thinly sliced
2 c. shredded mozzarella or
   Cheddar cheese
16-oz. pkg. bowtie pasta, cooked

In a skillet over medium-high heat, sauté sausage in butter until browned. Add chicken to skillet with sausage; stir well. Transfer sausage mixture to an ungreased 13"x9" baking pan; add mixed vegetables, onion, celery and green pepper. Top with cheese; cover with aluminum foil. Bake at 350 degrees for about 30 minutes, until vegetables are crisp-tender and cheese is melted. To serve, ladle sausage mixture over cooked pasta. Serves 8.

It's easy to separate frozen vegetables. Put them in a colander and pour on hot water. Let water drain into the sink and add veggies to casserole ingredients.

Baked Chicken Jambalaya

Pioneer Beef Stew

## Pioneer Beef Stew

*There's nothing more satisfying than a hearty bowl of beef stew.*

14-1/2 oz. can petite diced
  tomatoes
1 c. water
3 T. quick-cooking tapioca,
  uncooked
2 t. sugar

1-1/2 t. salt
1/2 t. pepper
1-1/2 lbs. stew beef cubes
3 to 4 potatoes, peeled and cubed
4 carrots, peeled and thickly sliced
1 onion, diced

In a large bowl, combine tomatoes with juice, water, tapioca, sugar, salt and pepper. Mix well; stir in remaining ingredients. Pour into a greased 13"x9" baking pan. Cover and bake at 375 degrees for 1-1/2 to 2 hours, until beef and vegetables are tender. Serves 4 to 6.

41

Eat-it-all bread bowls make hearty stew extra special. Cut the tops off round loaves of bread and hollow out, then rub with olive oil and garlic. Pop bread bowls in the oven at 400 degrees for 10 minutes, or until crusty and golden. Ladle in stew and enjoy!

## Butter-Roasted Chicken

*You'll love this savory golden chicken...it's oh-so flavorful, yet takes little effort to prepare.*

10 bone-in chicken thighs
1 c. water
1/2 c. lemon juice
2 T. butter, sliced
2 T. paprika
2 t. brown sugar, packed

2 t. salt
1 t. pepper
1 t. dried rosemary
1 t. chicken bouillon granules
1/4 t. cayenne pepper
1/4 t. nutmeg

Arrange chicken in an ungreased 13"x9" baking pan; set aside. Combine remaining ingredients in a small saucepan. Bring to a boil over medium-high heat; boil and stir for 2 minutes. Spoon mixture over chicken. Cover with aluminum foil; bake at 325 degrees for one hour. Uncover; baste chicken with pan drippings. Increase oven temperature to 450 degrees. Bake, uncovered, an additional 20 minutes, or until chicken is crisp and golden. Serves 5.

For a side dish that practically cooks itself, fill aluminum foil packets with sliced fresh veggies. Top with seasoning salt and 2 ice cubes; seal. Bake at 450 degrees for 20 to 25 minutes, or alongside a main dish at 350 degrees for a little longer. Delicious!

Butter-Roasted Chicken

## Turkey-Broccoli Casserole

*Feeding a crowd? This recipe will do the trick. Just add stuffing and cranberry sauce for a terrific meal.*

16-oz. pkg. frozen broccoli
2 lbs. ground turkey
8-oz. pkg. sliced mushrooms
1 onion, chopped
salt and pepper to taste

2 10-3/4 oz. cans cream of celery
  soup
16-oz. container sour cream
16-oz. pkg. shredded Monterey
  Jack cheese

Cook broccoli according to package directions; drain well. Meanwhile, in a large deep skillet over medium heat, brown turkey with mushrooms and onion; drain. Season turkey mixture with salt and pepper; stir in soup and sour cream. Reduce heat to low; heat through. Transfer turkey mixture to a lightly greased 13"x9" baking pan. Layer evenly with broccoli; top with cheese. Bake, uncovered, at 350 degrees for one hour, or until bubbly and lightly golden. Makes 8 to 10 servings.

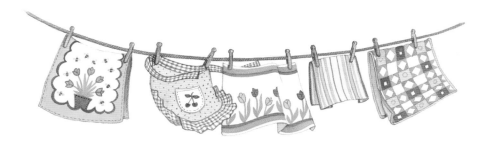

A ready-to-serve casserole is ideal for sharing with a new mom or new neighbor. For an extra-nice surprise, tuck a few favorite recipes inside an oven mitt and give along with the casserole.

## Eggplant Parmesan

*A hearty meatless dish that's perfect to enjoy with family & friends, no matter what the occasion. Serve over spaghetti.*

4 eggs, beaten
3 T. water
2 eggplants, peeled and sliced
   1/4-inch thick
2 c. Italian-style dry bread crumbs
1-1/2 c. grated Parmesan cheese,
   divided

28-oz. jar garden-style pasta
   sauce, divided
1-1/2 c. shredded mozzarella
   cheese

Whisk together eggs and water in a shallow bowl. Dip eggplant slices into egg mixture. Arrange slices in a single layer on a greased baking sheet. Bake, uncovered, at 350 degrees for 25 minutes, or until tender. Set aside. In a separate bowl, mix bread crumbs and 1/2 cup Parmesan cheese; set aside. Spread a small amount of sauce in an ungreased 13"x9" baking pan; layer with half the eggplant, one cup sauce, 1/2 cup remaining Parmesan cheese and one cup crumb mixture. Repeat layering. Cover with aluminum foil and bake for 45 minutes. Remove foil; sprinkle with mozzarella cheese. Bake, uncovered, for an additional 10 minutes. Serves 6 to 8.

A fresh salad is right at home alongside cheesy baked pasta casseroles. Toss together mixed greens, cherry tomatoes and thinly sliced red onion in a salad bowl. Whisk together 1/4 cup each of balsamic vinegar and olive oil, then drizzle over salad...so zesty!

Eggplant Parmesan

Beef & Bean Burritos

## Beef & Bean Burritos

*Ready in a jiffy! Add some warm cornbread or crunchy corn chips and dinner is served.*

1 lb. ground beef
1 onion, chopped
16-oz. can refried beans
1-1/4 oz. pkg. taco seasoning mix
1/2 c. water

12 10-inch flour tortillas
8-oz. jar taco sauce
16-oz. jar picante sauce
1-1/2 c. favorite shredded cheese

Brown beef and onion in a skillet over medium heat; drain. Add beans, seasoning mix and water; simmer until heated through. Meanwhile, place tortillas between dampened paper towels. Microwave on high setting for 30 to 60 seconds, until warm. Divide beef mixture evenly among tortillas; roll up. Place burritos seam-side down in a lightly greased 13"x9" baking pan. Mix sauces together; spoon evenly over burritos. Microwave, uncovered, on high for about 10 minutes, until hot and bubbly. Top with cheese; let stand until cheese melts. Serves 6, 2 burritos each.

49

Homemade guacamole is scrumptious and so easy to make. Cut 4 ripe avocados in half, remove the pits and scoop into a bowl. Add a chopped onion, 2 minced garlic cloves, 2 tablespoons lime juice and a dash of salt. Mash it up and serve...it can't be beat!

## Black Bean & Rice Enchiladas

*You won't even miss the meat with these flavor-packed enchiladas.*

1 green pepper, chopped
1/4 c. onion, chopped
3 cloves garlic, minced
1 T. olive oil
15-oz. can black beans, drained
  and rinsed
14-1/4 oz. can diced tomatoes with
  green chiles
1/4 c. taco sauce

1 T. chili powder
1 t. ground cumin
1/4 t. red pepper flakes
2 c. cooked brown rice
8 10-inch flour tortillas
1 c. salsa
1 c. shredded Cheddar cheese
3 T. fresh cilantro, chopped

In a skillet over medium heat, sauté green pepper, onion and garlic in oil until tender. Add beans, tomatoes with juice, taco sauce and seasonings. Simmer until heated through and mixture thickens. Stir in cooked rice; simmer for 5 minutes. Spoon filling down the center of each tortilla. Roll up tortillas; place in a lightly greased 13"x9" baking pan. Spoon salsa over enchiladas. Bake, covered, at 350 degrees for 25 minutes. Uncover; sprinkle with cheese and cilantro. Bake an additional 3 minutes, or until cheese is melted. Makes 8 servings.

Add authentic south-of-the-border flavor to Mexican dishes with quesadilla cheese or crumbly queso fresco, now stocked in many supermarkets. Can't find them? Monterey Jack is a good substitute.

Black Bean & Rice Enchiladas

Ham & Cheese Spaghetti

# Square Meals

## Ham & Cheese Spaghetti

*Real comfort food...a great way to make something delicious with leftover ham.*

1 lb. cooked ham, cubed
1 to 2 t. olive oil
1 green pepper, diced
1 onion, diced
2 to 3 cloves garlic, pressed

15-oz. can tomato sauce
14-1/2 oz. can diced tomatoes
Italian seasoning to taste
16-oz. pkg. spaghetti, uncooked
16-oz. pkg. sliced American cheese

In a skillet over medium heat, lightly brown ham in oil. Add pepper and onion; sauté until tender. Stir in garlic, tomato sauce, tomatoes with juice and seasoning; bring to a boil. Reduce heat; cover and simmer for 20 to 30 minutes, stirring occasionally. Meanwhile, cook spaghetti according to package directions; drain. In a greased 13"x9" baking pan, place a layer of spaghetti, a layer of ham mixture and 3 to 4 cheese slices. Repeat layering 2 to 3 times, ending with sauce and cheese. Bake, uncovered, at 375 degrees for about 10 minutes, until hot and bubbly. Serves 4 to 6.

## Cheddar Baked Spaghetti

*An easy recipe that's meatless and flavorful.*

16-oz. pkg. thin spaghetti,
  uncooked
1/2 c. butter, softened
16-oz. jar double Cheddar cheese
  pasta sauce

12-oz. can tomato paste
2 T. sugar
1/3 c. Italian-flavored dry bread
  crumbs

Cook pasta according to package directions, just until tender. Drain; return to cooking pot. Add butter; toss spaghetti until butter melts. Stir in pasta sauce, tomato paste and sugar. Transfer to a greased 13"x9" baking pan; sprinkle with bread crumbs. Bake, uncovered, at 350 degrees for 35 minutes, or until bubbly and topping is crunchy. Serves 6 to 8.

Laughter is brightest where food is best.
-Irish Proverb

## Chicken Parmesan

*Just six ingredients, but so yummy! Jazz it up with your favorite flavor of pasta sauce...there are lots to choose from.*

1 egg, beaten
3/4 c. Italian-seasoned dry bread crumbs
4 boneless, skinless chicken breasts

26-oz. jar pasta sauce
1 c. shredded mozzarella cheese
cooked spaghetti

Place egg and bread crumbs in separate shallow dishes. Dip chicken into egg, then into bread crumbs. Arrange chicken in a greased 13"x9" baking pan. Bake, uncovered, at 400 degrees for 30 minutes. Spoon pasta sauce over chicken and top with cheese. Bake another 15 minutes, or until chicken juices run clear. Serve chicken and sauce over spaghetti. Makes 4 servings.

For an elegant yet quick last-minute appetizer, toss a drained jar of Italian antipasto mix with bite-size cubes of mozzarella or provolone cheese. Serve with cocktail picks.

Chicken Parmesan

Little Meatloaves

## Little Meatloaves

*Italian-style meatloaf for a family of four in less than half an hour?*
*Oh, yes!*

1 egg, lightly beaten
1 c. pasta sauce, divided
1/2 c. dry bread crumbs
1/4 t. salt
4 T. fresh basil, coarsely chopped
  and divided

1 lb. ground beef
1 c. shredded mozzarella cheese,
  divided

In a large bowl, combine egg, 1/2 cup pasta sauce, bread crumbs, salt and 2 tablespoons basil. Add beef and 1/2 cup cheese. Mix well and shape into 4 ovals, each 5-1/2 by 2-inch. Place in a lightly greased 13"x9" baking pan. Spoon remaining sauce over meatloaves and sprinkle with remaining cheese. Bake, uncovered, at 450 degrees for 15 minutes. Sprinkle with remaining basil. Serves 4.

Pick up a package of refrigerated mashed potatoes at the grocery for a quick & easy side dish. Heat and stir in butter and sour cream to taste... as yummy as homemade, and a lot quicker!

## Swiss & Halibut Bake

*Topped with a creamy cheese sauce, this is a speedy yet elegant supper to share with friends.*

2 lbs. halibut fillets
1 T. lemon juice
3/4 c. white wine or chicken broth
salt and pepper to taste
1/4 lb. sliced mushrooms

1/4 c. butter
3 T. all-purpose flour
1 c. half-and-half
1/2 t. salt
1 c. shredded Swiss cheese

Arrange fish in a lightly greased 13"x9" baking pan. Drizzle with lemon juice and wine or broth; season with salt and pepper. Cover and bake at 400 degrees for 12 to 15 minutes, until fish flakes easily with a fork. Remove from oven; drain, reserving liquid. Meanwhile, in a skillet over medium heat, sauté mushrooms in butter; stir in flour. Add half-and-half and reserved liquid to skillet; cook and stir until thickened and smooth. Add salt and cheese; stir until cheese melts. Spoon sauce over fish. Bake, uncovered, for about 10 minutes. Serves 4 to 6.

## Baked Flounder & Tomatoes

*Delicious and so easy to prepare! Mahi-mahi and snapper are excellent in this recipe too.*

2 ripe tomatoes, sliced
salt and pepper to taste
chopped fresh dill to taste
1 c. Italian-seasoned dry bread
   crumbs, divided

1-1/2 lbs. flounder fillets
1/4 c. butter, melted
1/4 c. grated Parmesan cheese
paprika to taste

Arrange tomato slices in a lightly greased 13"x9" baking pan. Season lightly with salt and pepper; sprinkle with dill and 1/2 cup bread crumbs. Arrange fish fillets over tomatoes; season with salt and pepper. Top with more dill and remaining bread crumbs. Drizzle with melted butter; sprinkle with Parmesan cheese and paprika. Bake, uncovered, at 425 degrees for 10 to 15 minutes, just until fish flakes easily with a fork. Makes 6 servings.

Swiss & Halibut Bake

Greek Tilapia with Orzo

## Greek Tilapia with Orzo

*Try this tasty recipe with other fish, such as flounder, sole and perch too.*

1-1/2 lbs. tilapia fillets
juice and zest of 1 lemon
1 T. fresh oregano, snipped
salt and pepper to taste

1 pt. cherry tomatoes, halved
8-oz. pkg. orzo pasta, cooked
Optional: crumbled feta cheese

Rinse fish fillets and pat dry. Place in a lightly greased 13"x9" baking pan. Sprinkle fish evenly with lemon juice and zest, oregano, salt and pepper. Arrange tomatoes around fish; cover with aluminum foil. Bake at 400 degrees for 16 to 18 minutes, until fish is opaque and tomatoes are tender. Serve over cooked orzo, drizzled with juices from baking pan. Garnish with feta cheese, if desired. Serves 4.

Bake fish fillets in parchment paper for a delicious dinner with no fuss. Season fish and place on a sheet of parchment paper. Fold up the sides and crimp to make a tight package and place in a baking pan. Bake as usual, then slice open package and serve fish with its juices. Afterwards, just toss away the paper.

## Crab & Shrimp Casserole

*The yummy taste of the sea in a convenient casserole!*

2  8-oz. cans crabmeat, drained
2  4-oz. cans tiny shrimp, drained
2 c. celery, chopped
1 green pepper, chopped
1 onion, chopped
1 T. Worcestershire sauce
1 t. sugar

1 c. mayonnaise
salt and pepper to taste
1 c. soft bread crumbs
2 t. butter, melted
2 T. lemon juice
Garnish: thinly sliced lemon

In a bowl, mix together all ingredients except bread crumbs, butter, lemon juice and garnish. Transfer to a greased 13"x9" baking pan; set aside. In a separate bowl, toss bread crumbs with butter; spread over crabmeat mixture. Bake, uncovered, at 350 degrees for 30 to 40 minutes, until heated through. Drizzle with lemon juice; garnish with lemon slices. Serves 4 to 6.

Drizzle lemon-dill butter over warm rolls...great served with seafood dishes! Slowly melt one cup butter in a small saucepan over low heat. Skim off and discard white foam. Pour butter into a medium size bowl, then stir in one tablespoon chopped fresh dill and the zest of one lemon.

Crab & Shrimp Casserole

Turn any casserole into an overnight time-saver. Simply prepare a favorite recipe the night before, cover and refrigerate. The next day, just add 15 to 20 extra minutes to the baking time.

Sharing a casserole with a new mom? Bake it in a pretty speckled enamelware pan and make the pan part of her gift. It's sure to come in handy for lots of family dinners!

Shopping for a new casserole dish? Consider getting a deep 13"x9" glass baking pan. It retains heat well to create crisp golden crusts, cleans up easily and can be used for both savory mains and sweet desserts.

Packing a tomato-based casserole to share with a friend? Tuck in a small can of tomato juice too. Add a note to drizzle the juice over the casserole just before reheating...the casserole will be extra moist and flavorful.

# Potluck
# Pleasers

## Taco Lasagna

*A hearty lasagna that's just a little different! It freezes well too, so it's a great make-ahead. Wrap the unbaked lasagna well and freeze up to three months. To serve, thaw overnight and bake as directed.*

12 lasagna noodles, uncooked
1 lb. ground beef chuck
1-1/4 oz. pkg. taco seasoning mix
2 egg whites, beaten

15-oz. container ricotta cheese
16-oz. pkg. finely shredded
  Colby Jack cheese, divided
24-oz. jar salsa, divided

Cook noodles according to package directions, just until tender; drain. Meanwhile, brown beef in a skillet over medium heat; drain. Stir in taco seasoning, adding a small amount of water if a thinner sauce is desired. Remove from heat. In a bowl, combine egg whites and ricotta cheese until well blended. Lightly spray a deep 13"x9" baking pan with non-stick vegetable spray. Layer 4 noodles, 3/4 cup cheese mixture, half of beef mixture and 1-1/3 cups shredded cheese. Next, layer with 4 noodles, 3/4 cup cheese mixture, remaining beef mixture, 1-1/2 cups salsa and 1-1/3 cups shredded cheese. Layer with remaining noodles, cheese mixture, salsa and shredded cheese. Bake, uncovered, at 350 degrees for about 40 minutes, until hot and bubbly. Let stand for 10 minutes before serving. Makes 8 servings.

Feeding a crowd? Consider serving festive Mexican or Italian dishes that everybody loves. They often feature pasta or tortillas, so they're filling yet budget-friendly. The theme makes it a snap to put together the menu and table decorations too.

Taco Lasagna

Sloppy Joe Bake

# Potluck Pleasers

## Sloppy Joe Bake

*Sloppy Joes you can eat with a knife & fork...*
*all of the flavor, but less mess!*

1-1/2 lbs. ground beef
1/4 c. onion, chopped
1/4 c. green pepper, chopped
15-1/2 oz. can Sloppy Joe sauce
8-oz. pkg. shredded Cheddar
  cheese

2 c. biscuit baking mix
2 eggs, beaten
1 c. milk

In a skillet over medium heat, brown beef, onion and green pepper; drain.
Stir in sauce. Spoon mixture into a greased 13"x9" baking pan; sprinkle
with cheese. In a bowl, stir together remaining ingredients just until
blended. Spoon over cheese. Bake, uncovered, at 400 degrees for about
25 minutes, until golden. Cut into squares. Serves 8.

## Grandma's Baked Mac & Cheese

*A real crowd-pleaser...and you don't even have to precook the macaroni.*

2 c. elbow macaroni, uncooked
2-1/2 c. shredded sharp Cheddar
  cheese, divided

4 c. milk
salt and pepper to taste

In a greased 13"x9" baking pan, mix uncooked macaroni, 1/2 cup cheese,
milk, salt and pepper. Sprinkle remaining cheese over top. Bake, uncovered,
at 375 degrees for 45 minutes to one hour, until bubbly, golden and
macaroni is tender. Serves 8.

Take time to share family stories with your kids over the dinner table. A
cherished family recipe can be a super conversation starter.

## Creamy Chicken Bake

*Stir in some sliced mushrooms and diced green pepper, if you like.*

2 c. elbow macaroni, uncooked
1 c. mayonnaise
10-3/4 oz. can cream of chicken
  soup
1-1/2 c. cooked chicken, chopped

2 c. grated Parmesan cheese
1/4 c. chopped pimentos, drained
1/4 c. onion, chopped
1/2 c. potato chips, crushed

Cook macaroni according to package instructions; drain. Meanwhile, in a bowl, combine mayonnaise, soup and chicken. Stir in cooked macaroni and remaining ingredients except potato chips. Transfer mixture to a lightly greased 13"x9" baking pan; sprinkle with potato chips. Bake, uncovered, at 375 degrees for 30 minutes, or until hot and bubbly. Serves 4 to 6.

Cooking for a few? Divide a 13"x9" pan recipe between two 8"x8" pans. Enjoy one dish for dinner tonight, and freeze the other for a future no-fuss meal!

Creamy Chicken Bake

Creamy Chicken Enchiladas

## Creamy Chicken Enchiladas

*Pick up a roasted deli chicken to jump-start this yummy dinner favorite.*

2 c. cooked chicken, shredded
1 c. green pepper, diced
16-oz. jar picante sauce, divided
8-oz. pkg. cream cheese, softened
10 8-inch flour tortillas
16-oz. pkg. Mexican pasteurized
  process cheese spread, cubed

1/4 c. milk
2 2-1/4 oz. cans sliced black
  olives, drained
Garnish: salsa, guacamole,
  sour cream

In a skillet over low heat, cook and stir chicken, green pepper, one cup picante sauce and cream cheese until smooth. Spoon 1/4 cup of chicken mixture onto each tortilla. Roll up and place seam-side down in an ungreased 13"x9" baking pan; set aside. In the same skillet over low heat, cook and stir cubed cheese spread with milk until melted and smooth; spoon over enchiladas. Sprinkle olives on top; spoon remaining picante sauce over enchiladas. Cover with aluminum foil. Bake at 350 degrees for 25 minutes, or until heated through. Serve with salsa, guacamole and sour cream on the side. Makes 5 servings, 2 enchiladas each.

## Baked Swiss Chicken

*Tasty with a side of steamed and buttered broccoli.*

8 boneless, skinless chicken
  breasts
8 slices Swiss cheese
1/4 c. white wine or chicken broth

10-3/4 oz. can cream of
  chicken soup
3/4 c. herb-flavored stuffing mix
1/4 c. butter, melted

Arrange chicken in a greased 13"x9" baking pan; top each piece with a slice of cheese. In a bowl, combine wine or broth and soup; mix well and spoon over chicken. Sprinkle with stuffing and drizzle with butter. Bake, uncovered, at 350 degrees for 45 to 50 minutes, until chicken juices run clear when pierced. Makes 8 servings.

## Chile Relleno Casserole

*Tasty at breakfast, lunch or anytime!*

7-oz. can whole green chiles, drained
16-oz. pkg. shredded Monterey Jack cheese, divided
16-oz. pkg. shredded Cheddar cheese, divided

7-oz. can chopped green chiles
salt and pepper to taste
6 eggs, beaten
13-oz. can evaporated milk
Optional: salsa, sour cream

Slit whole chiles open and remove seeds; rinse and pat dry. Lay whole chiles, skin-side down, in a lightly greased 13"x9" baking pan; sprinkle with half of each cheese. Top with chopped chiles, remaining cheese, salt and pepper. In a bowl, whisk together eggs and milk; pour over top. Bake, uncovered, at 350 degrees for 45 minutes, or until hot and bubbly. Serve with salsa and sour cream, if desired. Serves 8.

Taking a casserole to a get-together? Wrap a pretty bandanna around the covered baking dish and slip the serving spoon inside the knot... keeps it right at your fingertips!

Chile Relleno Casserole

Lasagna Florentine

## Lasagna Florentine

*Extra-special lasagna...all dressed up with three kinds of cheese and good enough for company!*

1 lb. ground beef
1/2 c. onion, chopped
2 to 3 cloves garlic, minced
26-oz. jar spaghetti sauce, divided
16-oz. container cottage cheese
10-oz. pkg. frozen spinach, thawed and drained
12-oz. pkg. shredded mozzarella cheese, divided
1/2 c. grated Parmesan cheese, divided
2 eggs, beaten
9 lasagna noodles, cooked

Brown beef, onion and garlic in a skillet over medium heat. Drain; stir in spaghetti sauce and set aside. In a large bowl, combine cottage cheese, spinach, 2 cups mozzarella cheese, 1/4 cup Parmesan cheese and eggs. In an ungreased 13"x9" baking pan, layer one cup sauce mixture, 3 lasagna noodles and 1/2 cup cottage cheese mixture; repeat layers once. Top with remaining 3 noodles, sauce mixture, mozzarella and Parmesan. Cover with aluminum foil; bake at 350 degrees for 30 minutes. Uncover; bake for an additional 15 minutes. Let stand for 10 minutes before slicing. Makes 9 servings.

77

Cook lasagna noodles the easy way! Put them in a baking pan filled with very hot water while mixing up the rest of the recipe. They will be soft and pliable when you're ready for them!

## Sausage & Apple Kraut

*Serve with mashed potatoes, buttered green beans and fresh-baked rolls for a satisfying chilly-weather meal.*

27-oz. jar sauerkraut, drained, rinsed and divided
1 lb. Kielbasa sausage, sliced and divided
2 tart apples, peeled, cored and diced
1/2 c. brown sugar, packed and divided
2 c. apple cider or juice, divided

In a lightly greased 13"x9" baking pan, layer half of sauerkraut, half of sausage and all the apples. Sprinkle with 1/4 cup brown sugar. Pour one cup cider or juice over top. Repeat layering. Cover and bake at 350 degrees for 1-1/2 hours, or until sauerkraut is caramelized and golden. Makes 4 to 6 servings.

Crispy potato pancakes are a great way to use leftover mashed potatoes. Stir an egg yolk and some minced onion into 2 cups potatoes. Form into patties and fry in butter until golden. Delicious with sausage!

Sausage & Apple Kraut

Deep-Dish Sausage Casserole

## Deep-Dish Sausage Casserole

*Why send out for pizza when you can feast on a hot pizza right from your own oven?*

16-oz. pkg. frozen bread dough, thawed
1 lb. sweet Italian pork sausage, casings removed
2 c. shredded mozzarella cheese
1 green pepper, diced
1 red pepper, diced
28-oz. can diced tomatoes, drained
3/4 t. dried oregano
1/4 t. garlic powder
1/2 t. salt
1/2 c. grated Parmesan cheese

Press dough into the bottom and up the sides of a greased 13"x9" baking pan; set aside. Crumble sausage into a large skillet over medium heat. Cook until no longer pink; drain. Sprinkle sausage over dough; top with mozzarella cheese. In the same skillet, sauté peppers until slightly tender. Stir in tomatoes and seasonings; spoon over pizza. Sprinkle with Parmesan cheese. Bake, uncovered, at 350 degrees for 25 to 35 minutes, until crust is golden. Makes 8 servings.

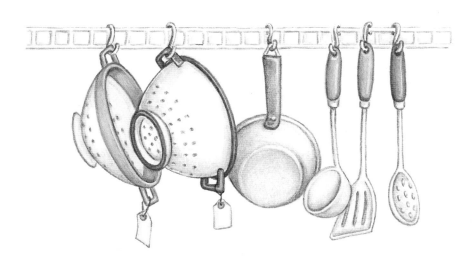

Serve an everyday meal on your best china and linens...
what are you saving them for?

## Easy-Cheesy Stuffed Shells

*Perfect when you're having a crowd for dinner. It's super easy and can be made up ahead of time...more time to spend with your guests!*

24 jumbo pasta shells, uncooked
1 lb. lean ground beef
26-oz. jar pasta sauce
1/4 c. water
1/2 c. grated Parmesan cheese

8-oz. container chive & onion
   cream cheese spread
2 c. shredded Italian-blend cheese,
   divided
1 egg, beaten

Cook pasta shells according to package directions, just until tender; drain. Meanwhile, brown beef in a skillet over medium heat; drain and cool slightly. In a bowl, mix pasta sauce and water. Spread one cup sauce mixture in an ungreased 13"x9" baking pan. In a separate bowl, mix Parmesan cheese, cheese spread, one cup Italian-blend cheese, egg and beef. Spoon a heaping tablespoonful of mixture into each shell. Arrange stuffed shells over sauce in pan. Spoon remaining sauce mixture over top, covering shells completely. Cover with aluminum foil. Bake at 350 degrees for 40 to 45 minutes, until bubbly. Sprinkle with remaining cheese; bake 10 minutes longer. Makes 8 to 10 servings.

## Spicy Baked Linguine

*Easy to assemble now and bake later...perfect for busy days.*

16-oz. pkg. linguine pasta,
   uncooked
1 T. oil
1 zucchini, cut into one-inch
   chunks

1 red pepper, cut into one-inch
   chunks
26-oz. jar spaghetti sauce
1 c. mild or medium salsa
3/4 c. shredded mozzarella cheese

Cook pasta according to package directions; drain. Meanwhile, heat oil in a stockpot over medium-high heat. Add zucchini and pepper; sauté for 6 to 8 minutes. Stir in spaghetti sauce and salsa. Add cooked pasta; mix well. Transfer to a lightly greased 13"x9" baking pan. Sprinkle with cheese. Bake, uncovered, at 350 degrees for 25 to 30 minutes. Serves 6 to 8.

Easy-Cheesy Stuffed Shells

Inside-Out Ravioli

# Potluck Pleasers

## Inside-Out Ravioli

*Just add a crisp tossed salad with oil & vinegar dressing for a hearty Italian-style meal. Please pass the Parmesan!*

16-oz. pkg. small shell or bowtie
   pasta, uncooked
1 lb. ground beef
1 c. onion, chopped
1/2 c. dry bread crumbs
1 egg, beaten
1 t. Italian seasoning
1 t. salt

1 t. pepper
8-oz. pkg. sliced mushrooms
10-oz. pkg. frozen chopped
   spinach, thawed and drained
16-oz. jar spaghetti sauce
1 c. shredded mozzarella cheese
Garnish: grated Parmesan cheese

Cook pasta according to package directions; drain. Meanwhile, brown beef with onion in a skillet over medium heat; drain. In a greased 13"x9" baking pan, combine cooked pasta, beef mixture and remaining ingredients except sauce and cheeses. Stir gently; top with sauce and mozzarella cheese. Bake, uncovered, at 350 degrees for 45 minutes, or until hot and bubbly. Sprinkle with Parmesan cheese at serving time. Makes 10 servings.

## Super Bowl Brisket

*A game-day favorite that serves a crowd! Pile into crusty rolls and add your favorite toppings.*

2 2 to 3-lb. center-cut beef
   briskets, trimmed

8-oz. bottle Italian salad dressing
Montreal steak seasoning to taste

Place briskets in 2 large plastic zipping bags; pour dressing over top. Marinate, refrigerated, for 24 hours. Remove briskets from bags; discard marinade. Season briskets with steak seasoning; wrap tightly in aluminum foil. Place in an ungreased 13"x9" baking pan. Bake at 325 degrees for 3 hours. Reduce heat to 300 degrees; bake for another 1-1/2 to 2 hours. Let briskets stand, wrapped in foil, for about 15 minutes before serving. Slice to serve. Serves 8.

## Cranberry Chicken

*A family-favorite, quick-fix recipe just right for busy holiday evenings.*

8-oz. can whole-berry cranberry
  sauce
1 c. French salad dressing
1.35-oz. pkg. onion soup mix

8 boneless, skinless chicken
  breasts
1/4 t. pepper
4 c. cooked rice

In a bowl, combine cranberry sauce, salad dressing and soup mix. Spread half of the cranberry mixture in a greased 13"x9" baking pan. Arrange chicken in a single layer over sauce mixture. Season with pepper, then top with remaining cranberry mixture. Bake, covered, at 325 degrees for 35 to 45 minutes, until juices run clear when chicken is pierced. Serve over cooked rice. Serves 8.

Give a homemade taste to packaged stuffing mixes with very little effort. Sauté 1/4 cup each of chopped onion and celery, add to the stuffing mix and prepare as the package directs.

Cranberry Chicken

Crunchy Hot Chicken Salad

## Crunchy Hot Chicken Salad

*Serve with tropical fruit cups and buttered rolls for a delightful luncheon meal.*

6 T. butter, divided
1 c. celery, chopped
1/2 c. green pepper, diced
1/3 c. onion, chopped
2 to 3 T. diced pimentos, drained
4-oz. can sliced mushrooms,
   drained

2-1/4 oz. pkg. slivered almonds
4 c. cooked chicken, diced
1 c. mayonnaise
10-3/4 oz. can cream of celery
   soup
1 t. salt
1 c. corn flake cereal, crushed

Melt 4 tablespoons butter in a large skillet over medium heat; add vegetables and almonds. Sauté until tender; spoon into an ungreased 13"x9" baking pan. Add chicken, mayonnaise, soup and salt to pan; mix well. Melt remaining butter and toss with cereal; sprinkle over top. Bake, uncovered, at 350 degrees for 30 minutes. Makes 10 servings.

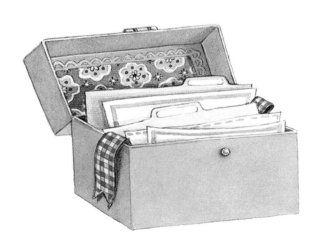

Make your ladies' luncheon a recipe swap! Invite friends to choose several of their best recipes to share, then make enough copies for everyone who will be coming. It's a fun way to pass along tried & true recipes, as well as enjoy a tasty lunch.

## Lattice Chicken Pot Pie

*This homestyle favorite looks so impressive, but the criss-cross crust is a snap to make with crescent rolls.*

1 to 2 boneless, skinless chicken breasts, cooked and cubed
4 c. frozen mixed vegetables, thawed
10-3/4 oz. can cream of chicken soup

10-3/4 oz. can cream of mushroom soup
1-1/2 t. dried rosemary
8-oz. tube refrigerated crescent rolls

In a large bowl, mix all ingredients except crescent rolls. Spoon into a lightly greased 13"x9" baking pan. Roll out crescent rolls without separating them; pinch gently to close seams. Cut dough lengthwise into one-inch wide strips. Criss-cross strips over pan in a lattice pattern. Bake at 350 degrees for one to 1-1/2 hours, until bubbly and crust is golden. Makes 6 servings.

Create a meal plan for one or even 2 weeks, including all of your favorite quick & easy meals...spaghetti on Monday, chicken pot pie on Tuesday and so forth. Post it on the fridge along with a shopping list, then making dinner will be a snap!

Lattice Chicken Pot Pie

Delectable Baked Chicken

# Potluck Pleasers

## Delectable Baked Chicken

*Serve with savory rice pilaf and steamed asparagus...*
*sure to be a hit at dinnertime!*

8 boneless, skinless chicken
  breasts
2 c. sour cream
1/4 c. lemon juice
4 t. Worcestershire sauce
1 T. garlic salt

2 t. paprika
2 t. salt
2 t. pepper
1-1/2 to 2 c. dry bread crumbs
1/2 c. butter, melted
1/2 c. oil

Arrange chicken in a lightly greased 13"x9" glass baking pan; set aside. In a bowl, combine sour cream, lemon juice, Worcestershire sauce and seasonings. Coat chicken evenly with sour cream mixture; cover and refrigerate overnight. About an hour before serving time, roll chicken in bread crumbs and return to pan. In a bowl, whisk together butter and oil; spoon half of mixture over chicken in pan. Bake, uncovered, at 350 degrees for 45 minutes. Spoon remaining butter mixture over chicken. Bake 15 minutes longer, just until chicken juices run clear when pierced. Makes 8 servings.

93

## Yummy Pork Ribs

*Delectable and oh-so-easy...perfect for a tailgating get-together!*

2 c. zesty Italian salad dressing
1/4 c. soy sauce
1 T. garlic, minced
1/2 t. pepper
4 lbs. bone-in country-style pork
  ribs

2 T. olive oil
2 to 3 onions, sliced and separated
  into rings

In a small bowl, stir together salad dressing, soy sauce, garlic and pepper; set aside. In a skillet over medium heat, brown ribs in oil on both sides; drain. Arrange onion rings in an ungreased 13"x9" baking pan. Top with ribs; drizzle ribs with dressing mixture. Cover tightly. Bake at 350 degrees for one hour, or until tender. Serves 6.

## Company Baked Ziti

*With layers of sour cream and two kinds of cheese, this pasta classic
is extra rich and cheesy. Try curly cavatappi or gemelli pasta
instead of ziti too.*

16-oz. pkg. ziti pasta, uncooked
1 lb. ground beef
1 lb. sweet Italian ground pork
  sausage
1 onion, chopped
2 26-oz. jars spaghetti sauce

16-oz. pkg. sliced provolone cheese
1 c. sour cream
1-1/2 c. shredded mozzarella
  cheese
1/2 c. grated Parmesan cheese

Cook pasta according to package directions, just until tender; drain.
Meanwhile, brown beef, sausage and onion in a skillet over medium heat;
drain. Stir in sauce; reduce heat to low and simmer for 15 minutes. In a
greased deep 13"x9" baking pan, layer half the cooked pasta, provolone
cheese, sour cream, half the sauce mixture, remaining pasta, mozzarella
cheese and remaining sauce. Top with Parmesan cheese. Cover and bake at
350 degrees for 30 minutes, or until hot, bubbly and cheeses are melted.
Serves 8.

94

For baked casseroles with pasta, cook pasta for the shortest cooking
time recommended on the package. It will finish cooking in the oven
and will hold its shape without becoming mushy.

Company Baked Ziti

Polenta Casserole

## Polenta Casserole

*Easy, filling and best of all, yummy!*

3 c. water
1 c. yellow cornmeal
1 t. salt
1/2 t. Montreal steak seasoning
1 c. shredded sharp Cheddar
   cheese, divided
1 lb. ground beef
1 c. onion, chopped

1 zucchini, halved lengthwise and
   sliced
1 T. olive oil
2 14-1/2 oz. cans diced tomatoes,
   drained
6-oz. can tomato paste
Garnish: fresh parsley, chopped

In a 2-quart saucepan, bring water to a boil. Whisk in cornmeal and salt; reduce heat to low. Simmer, whisking constantly, for 3 minutes, or until thickened. Remove from heat; stir in steak seasoning and 1/4 cup cheese. Spread cornmeal mixture in a greased 13"x9" baking pan; set aside. In a skillet over medium heat, brown beef with onion and zucchini in oil; drain. Stir in tomatoes and tomato paste; simmer for 10 minutes, stirring often. Spoon beef mixture over cornmeal mixture; sprinkle with remaining cheese. Bake, uncovered, at 350 degrees for 30 minutes, or until bubbly. Garnish with parsley. Serves 6.

Fresh mozzarella is delicious on baked pasta dishes but can be difficult to grate. Freeze it first! Wrap the ball of cheese in plastic wrap and freeze for 20 minutes, then grate. Store the grated cheese in a resealable plastic zipping bag in the refrigerator for up to 5 days.

## Macaroni & Cheese Deluxe

*A family favorite...it melts in your mouth, it's so good!*

3 c. elbow macaroni, uncooked
16-oz. container small-curd
  cottage cheese
8-oz. container sour cream
1 egg, beaten

3/4 t. pepper
1/2 t. garlic powder
8-oz. pkg. shredded Cheddar
  cheese
Optional: paprika

Cook macaroni according to package directions, just until tender; drain. In a bowl, combine cottage cheese, sour cream, egg and seasonings. Add Cheddar cheese and mix well; add macaroni and stir until coated. Transfer to a greased 13"x9" baking pan. Cover and bake at 350 degrees for 25 to 30 minutes, until heated through. Sprinkle with paprika, if desired. Makes 6 to 8 servings.

If you love macaroni & cheese with a chewy, crusty topping, but hate to scrub the baked-on cheese in the casserole dish afterwards, try this! Fill the dish with warm water and add a teaspoon or 2 of baking soda. Let stand overnight. The next day, the baked-on portion will loosen easily.

Macaroni & Cheese Deluxe

Bacon Cheeseburger Casserole

## Bacon Cheeseburger Casserole

*This easy-to-do meal will make the whole family happy.*

2 lbs. ground beef
1/2 t. salt
1/2 t. pepper
1/2 t. garlic salt
10-3/4 oz. can cream of mushroom
  soup

10-3/4 oz. can Cheddar cheese soup
1/2 lb. bacon, crisply cooked and
  crumbled
1/2 onion, thinly sliced
28-oz. pkg. frozen zesty French
  fries

Brown beef in a skillet over medium heat. Drain; stir in seasonings, soups and bacon. Spread beef mixture in a 13"x9" baking pan sprayed with non-stick vegetable spray. Layer onion and frozen fries over top. Bake, uncovered, at 350 degrees for 45 to 60 minutes, until bubbly and fries are golden. Makes 10 servings.

## Dad's Wimpy Burgers

*No standing over a hot grill! Burgers for the whole family, done to perfection. Toss a salad while they're baking.*

2 lbs. ground beef
1/2 c. catsup
1 egg, beaten
1 onion, chopped

1 t. salt
1 c. Italian-style dry bread crumbs
6 to 8 hamburger buns, split

In a large bowl, combine beef, catsup, egg, onion and salt; mix well. Form into 6 to 8 patties; flatten to desired thickness. Place bread crumbs in a shallow pan. Pat each side of patties in crumbs just to coat. Place patties in a lightly greased 13"x9" baking pan. Bake, uncovered, at 350 degrees for 20 to 25 minutes, turning over after 8 minutes. Serve in buns. Makes 6 to 8 servings.

A smile is a curve that sets everything straight.
-Phyllis Diller

## Ravioli Taco Bake

*So easy! Serve with a simple salad of lettuce, tomato and avocado.*

1-1/2 lbs. ground beef
1-1/4 oz. pkg. taco seasoning mix
3/4 c. water
40-oz. can meat-filled ravioli with
   sauce

8-oz. pkg. shredded Cheddar
   cheese
Optional: sliced black olives

Brown beef in a large skillet over medium heat; drain. Stir in seasoning mix and water. Reduce heat; simmer for 8 to 10 minutes. Meanwhile, arrange ravioli in a lightly greased 13"x9" baking pan. Spoon beef mixture over top; sprinkle with cheese. Bake, uncovered, at 350 degrees for 25 to 30 minutes, until bubbly and cheese is melted. If desired, sprinkle with olives before serving. Serves 6 to 8.

Take advantage of grocery specials on ground beef for easy family meals! Crumble several pounds of beef into a baking pan and bake at 350 degrees until browned through, stirring often. Drain well and pack recipe-size portions in freezer bags.

Ravioli Taco Bake

Taco Stacks

## Taco Stacks

*So simple to make...let the kids help with the layering!*

2 lbs. ground beef
1 onion, chopped
16-oz. can black beans, drained
    and rinsed
16-oz. can pinto beans, drained
    and rinsed

6 8-inch flour tortillas
26-oz. can tomato soup
1-1/2 c. shredded Cheddar cheese
Garnish: sour cream, salsa

Brown beef in a skillet over medium heat; drain. Stir in onion and beans; cook until onion is translucent. Place a tortilla in the bottom of a greased 13"x9" baking pan. Spoon 1/2 cup soup over tortilla; layer with beef mixture and sprinkle with 1/4 cup cheese. Repeat, making 4 layers; top with remaining tortilla, soup and cheese. Cover with aluminum foil; bake at 350 degrees for 30 minutes. Serve with sour cream and salsa. Serves 6.

A speedy side for any south-of-the-border supper. Stir spicy salsa and shredded cheese into hot cooked rice. Cover and let stand a few minutes, until the cheese melts. Sure to please!

## Easy Sweet-and-Sour Chicken

*Serve on a bed of steamed rice or crunchy chow mein noodles for a meal the whole family will love.*

8-oz. bottle Russian salad dressing
1-1/2 oz. pkg. onion soup mix
1/3 c. apricot jam

2-1/2 to 3 lbs. boneless, skinless
   chicken breasts
Garnish: chopped green onions

Whisk together salad dressing, soup mix and jam in a bowl; set aside. Arrange chicken in an ungreased 13"x9" baking pan; pour dressing mixture on top. Bake, covered, at 350 degrees for 50 minutes to one hour, until juices run clear when chicken is pierced. If desired, cut chicken into strips before serving; garnish with green onions. Makes 4 to 6 servings.

Cloth napkins are so much nicer than paper ones...why not whip up some fun napkin rings for them? Stitch a big vintage button or a pretty silk flower onto colorful new hair elastics...done in a snap!

Easy Sweet-and-Sour Chicken

Sunday Chicken & Dressin

## Sunday Chicken & Dressing

*So good! You'll love the aroma as this casserole bakes. Try it with leftover roast turkey too.*

2 6-oz. pkgs. chicken-flavored
   stuffing mix
10-3/4 oz. can cream of chicken
   soup
10-3/4 oz. can cream of celery or
   mushroom soup

1 c. chicken broth
2-1/2 to 3 lbs. cooked chicken,
   cubed and divided

Prepare stuffing mix according to package instructions; set aside. Meanwhile, combine soups and broth in a large bowl; whisk together and set aside. Arrange half of chicken in a lightly greased 13"x9" baking pan; top with half of prepared stuffing and half of soup mixture. Repeat layers, ending with soup mixture. Bake, uncovered, at 350 degrees for one hour, or until hot and bubbly. Makes 8 to 10 servings.

If a recipe calls for cooked chicken, use this tip for juicy, flavorful chicken. Cover with water and simmer gently until cooked through, then turn off the heat and let the chicken cool in its own broth. Even easier...pick up a roast chicken at the deli!

## Chili-Cornbread Salad

*Want a potluck salad that everyone will love? This is it! When sweet corn is in season, use it instead of the canned corn for even more flavor.*

8-1/2 oz. pkg. cornbread muffin
  mix
4-oz. can chopped green chiles
1/8 t. ground cumin
1/8 t. dried oregano
1/8 t. dried sage
1 c. mayonnaise
1 c. sour cream
1-oz. env. ranch salad
  dressing mix

2 15-oz. cans pinto beans, drained
2 15-1/2 oz. cans corn, drained
3 tomatoes, chopped
1 c. green pepper, chopped
1 c. onion, chopped
10 slices bacon, crisply cooked
  and crumbled
2 c. shredded Cheddar cheese

Prepare cornbread mix according to package directions; stir in chiles and seasonings. Spread batter in a greased 8"x8" baking pan. Bake at 400 degrees for 20 to 25 minutes, until center tests done; set aside to cool. In a small bowl, combine mayonnaise, sour cream and ranch dressing mix; set aside. Crumble half of the cornbread into a lightly greased 13"x9" glass baking pan. Layer with half each of beans, mayonnaise mixture, corn, tomatoes, green pepper, onion, bacon and cheese. Repeat layers. Cover and refrigerate for 2 hours. Serves 12.

Chili-Cornbread Salad

Chicken & Rice Salad

## Chicken & Rice Salad

*Scrumptious and so pretty, with the colors of red peppers, black olives, herbs and artichokes.*

3 T. red wine vinegar
1-1/2 T. extra-virgin olive oil
1/4 t. pepper
1 clove garlic, minced
2 c. long-grain rice, cooked
1-1/2 c. cooked chicken breast, diced
1/2 c. roasted red peppers, drained and diced
1/2 c. Kalamata olives, pitted and halved
1/4 c. fresh chives, chopped
1/4 c. fresh basil, chopped
1/4 c. fresh oregano, chopped
14-oz. can artichoke hearts, drained and diced
4-oz. pkg. crumbled feta cheese

In a small bowl, whisk together vinegar, olive oil, pepper and garlic; set aside. In a 13"x9" baking pan, combine cooked rice and remaining ingredients except cheese. At serving time, drizzle vinegar mixture over salad; sprinkle with cheese. Serve at room temperature or chilled. Makes 4 servings.

## Soft Sesame Bread Sticks

*Round out a meal with warm bread, made from scratch...it's simple!*

1-1/4 c. all-purpose flour
2 t. sugar
1-1/2 t. baking powder
1/2 t. salt
2/3 c. milk
3 T. butter, melted
2 t. sesame seed

In a small bowl, combine flour, sugar, baking powder and salt. Gradually add milk; stir to form a soft dough. Turn onto a floured surface; knead gently 3 to 4 times. Roll into a 10-inch by 5-1/2 inch rectangle; cut into 12 bread sticks. Place butter in a 13"x9" baking pan; coat bread sticks in butter and sprinkle with sesame seed. Bake at 450 degrees for 14 to 18 minutes, until golden. Makes one dozen.

Turn bread sticks into soft pretzels just for fun! Twist strips of dough into pretzel shapes and place on an ungreased baking sheet. Brush with beaten egg white, sprinkle with coarse salt and bake as directed.

## Marilyn's Spaghetti Salad

*A great dish for gatherings and picnics...easy to make
and packed with veggies.*

16-oz. pkg. spaghetti, uncooked
2 cucumbers, peeled, seeded and
    diced
2 tomatoes, diced
3 green onions, chopped
1/2 green pepper, chopped
1/2 red pepper, chopped
8-oz. bottle sun-dried tomato
    vinaigrette salad dressing
salt and pepper to taste

Cook spaghetti according to package directions; drain and rinse with cold
water. In a 13"x9" glass baking pan, combine spaghetti and vegetables. Add
salad dressing; toss gently to coat well. Cover and refrigerate several hours
to overnight. Season with salt and pepper at serving time. Serves 8.

When it's just too hot to cook, invite friends and neighbors over for a
salad potluck. You set up a table in a shady spot and set out pitchers of
ice tea...everyone brings along their favorite salad to share.

Marilyn's Spaghetti Salad

Carrying a dish to a potluck or get-together? Help the hosts keep track of dishes by taping a label to the bottom of your pan. Be sure to use a waterproof marker and include your name and phone number.

For a crispy, crunchy casserole topping, leave the pan uncovered while it's baking. Cover it only if you prefer a softer consistency.

Lots of different pasta shapes like bowties, seashells and corkscrew-shaped cavatappi work well in casseroles...why not give a favorite casserole a whole new look?

First aid for pans with baked-on food spatters! Mix equal amounts of cream of tartar and white vinegar into a paste. Spread onto the pan and let stand for 30 minutes to an hour. Spatters will wash off easily.

# Toss-Together Sides

## Sweet Corn & Rice Casserole

*Roll up leftovers in a flour tortilla for a hearty snack.*

2 T. butter
1 green pepper, chopped
1 onion, chopped
15-1/2 oz. can creamed corn
11-oz. can sweet corn & diced
   peppers, drained
11-oz. can corn, drained
6 c. cooked rice

10-oz. can diced tomatoes with
   green chiles, drained
8-oz. pkg. mild Mexican
   pasteurized process cheese
   spread, cubed
1/2 t. salt
1/4 t. pepper
1/2 c. shredded Cheddar cheese

Melt butter in a large skillet over medium heat. Add green pepper and onion; sauté 5 minutes, or until tender. Stir in remaining ingredients except shredded cheese; spoon into a lightly greased 13"x9" baking pan. Bake, uncovered, at 350 degrees for 25 to 30 minutes, until heated through. Top with shredded cheese; bake an additional 5 minutes, or until cheese melts. Makes 10 to 12 servings.

Steamed rice that's tender...never mushy! Cook long-cooking rice according to package directions. When it's done, remove pan from heat, cover with a folded tea towel and replace the lid. Let stand for 5 to 10 minutes, fluff with a fork and serve. The towel will absorb any excess moisture.

Sweet Corn & Rice Casserole

Green Bean Delight

## Green Bean Delight

*An old standby dressed up with shredded cheese and nuts.*

4 16-oz. cans green beans, drained
1-oz. pkg. ranch salad dressing
  mix
2 10-3/4 oz. cans cream of
  mushroom soup

1/4 c. milk
8-oz. pkg. shredded Colby Jack
  cheese
1 c. sliced almonds or cashews
2.8-oz. can French fried onions

Spread green beans in a lightly greased 13"x9" baking pan; set aside.
Combine salad dressing mix, soup and milk in a bowl; drizzle over beans.
Sprinkle with cheese, nuts and onions. Bake, uncovered, at 350 degrees
for 25 minutes. Serves 8 to 10.

Keep a permanent marker handy in the kitchen to write the
purchase date on food cans and packages...you'll always know
which ones to use first.

## Scalloped Potatoes

*Just about every grandma had her own recipe for delicious scalloped potatoes. This one is extra yummy, with bacon and cheese!*

3 potatoes, peeled and sliced
6 slices bacon, halved
1 onion, chopped
3 T. fried chicken coating mix
1/2 t. salt
2 c. milk
1 c. shredded Cheddar cheese

In a saucepan over medium heat, cover potatoes with water. Cook until almost tender; drain. Meanwhile, cook bacon and onion in a skillet over medium heat. Drain and set aside bacon mixture, reserving 2 tablespoons drippings. Add coating mix, salt and milk to reserved drippings; cook until thickened. Fold potatoes into bacon mixture. Transfer to a greased 13"x9" baking pan. Cover and bake at 350 degrees for 30 minutes. Uncover; top with cheese and bake for another 15 minutes, or until cheese is melted. Serves 6.

## Savory Baked Potatoes

*Looking for something different in a potato dish? This is easy and delicious.*

5 to 6 russet potatoes, very thinly
   sliced and divided
1/4 c. extra-virgin olive oil, divided
2 t. garlic powder
2 t. seasoned salt
1/2 t. celery salt
2 t. salt
2 t. pepper
dried parsley to taste

Arrange half of the potato slices in a greased 13"x9" glass baking pan. Drizzle with half of the oil; sprinkle with half of all seasonings except parsley. Repeat layers; sprinkle parsley on top. Cover with aluminum foil. Bake at 375 degrees for 35 to 45 minutes, until potatoes are tender. Serves 6.

Tuck packets of salad and seasoning mix into a small enamel pail to keep the pantry tidy.

Scalloped Potatoes

Scalloped Corn

## Scalloped Corn

*Seems like it isn't a family reunion unless this dish is on the buffet!*

1 onion, chopped
1/2 c. plus 1 T. butter, melted
14-3/4 oz. can creamed corn
2  11-oz. cans corn, drained

8-1/2 oz. pkg. corn muffin mix
dried parsley, salt and pepper
   to taste

In a skillet over medium heat, sauté onion in butter until translucent. Transfer onion mixture to a  lightly greased 13"x9" baking pan; stir in remaining ingredients. Bake, uncovered, at 350 degrees for 45 minutes to one hour, until bubbly and golden. Serves 8.

Fresh sweet corn makes any corn recipe more delicious! When cutting the kernels from ears of corn, stand the ear in the center of a tube cake pan. The kernels will fall neatly into the pan.

# Toss-Together Sides

## Mexican Veggie Bake

*Layers of tasty sautéed fresh vegetables and melted cheese...
perfect for a meatless Monday.*

1/2 c. green pepper, finely chopped
1/2 c. carrot, peeled and finely
  chopped
1/2 c. celery, finely chopped
1/2 c. onion, finely chopped
2 c. cooked rice

16-oz. can refried beans
15-oz. can black beans, drained
  and rinsed
1 c. salsa
12-oz. pkg. shredded Cheddar
  cheese, divided

Sauté vegetables in a lightly greased skillet over medium heat until tender,
about 5 minutes. Transfer vegetables to a large bowl; add remaining
ingredients except cheese. Layer half of mixture in a lightly greased
13"x9" baking pan; sprinkle with half of cheese. Repeat layering, ending
with cheese. Bake, uncovered, at 350 degrees until heated through, about
15 to 20 minutes. Serves 6.

## Nonnie's Baked Zucchini

*Too many zucchini in the garden? Not when you have
this yummy recipe handy!*

8 zucchini, halved lengthwise
1/2 onion, chopped
1 to 2 t. oil
2 eggs, beaten
1 c. cottage cheese
1/2 c. buttermilk

salt and pepper to taste
1/2 c. shredded Cheddar cheese
1 c. toasted bread crumbs
paprika to taste
Garnish: chopped fresh parsley

Place zucchini in a lightly greased 13"x9" glass baking pan, cut-side
up. Cover and bake at 350 degrees until partially tender, about 15 to
20 minutes; remove from oven. Meanwhile, in a small skillet, sauté onion
in oil; drain. Beat together eggs, cottage cheese, buttermilk, salt and pepper;
stir in onion mixture. Spoon over zucchini. Sprinkle with shredded cheese
and bread crumbs; dust with paprika. Bake for an additional 15 minutes.
Garnish with parsley. Serves 8 to 10.

Mexican Veggie Bake

Cowboy Cornbread

## Cowboy Cornbread

*Bake up a pan of this extra special cornbread for your next chili supper...
they'll love it!*

2 c. biscuit baking mix
1 c. yellow cornmeal
3/4 c. sugar
1-1/2 t. baking powder
1/2 t. salt

2 eggs, beaten
1 c. half-and-half
1 c. butter, melted and slightly
  cooled

In a bowl, mix together biscuit mix, cornmeal, sugar, baking powder and
salt. Add remaining ingredients; stir until well blended. Pour batter into a
greased 13"x9" baking pan. Bake at 350 degrees for 25 to 30 minutes.
Cut into squares; serve warm. Makes 12 to 15 servings.

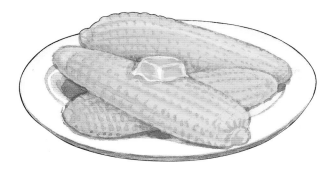

Add a delicious surprise to a favorite cornbread recipe...try fresh corn,
chopped green chiles or red peppers, crumbled bacon or snipped
fresh chives.

## Baked Stuffed Tomatoes

*Rediscover this old-fashioned favorite...it's as scrumptious as ever!*

8 ripe tomatoes
1 c. dry bread crumbs
4 t. butter, melted
2 t. grated Parmesan cheese

1 t. dried basil
1 t. dried oregano
4 t. fresh parsley, finely chopped
salt and pepper to taste

Slice tops off tomatoes; set aside. Scoop out some of the pulp from tomatoes; discard. Blend together remaining ingredients. Spoon crumb mixture evenly into each tomato, pressing firmly. Place tomatoes in a greased 13"x9" baking pan. Bake, uncovered, at 350 degrees for 20 minutes, or until topping is golden. Makes 8 servings.

## Fancy Sunday Squash Dish

*You'll love this creamy casserole with its golden crumb topping.*

2 lbs. yellow squash, chopped
1/2 c. onion, chopped
1/2 c. water
8-oz. container sour cream
salt and pepper to taste
1/4 t. dried basil

1 c. soft bread crumbs
1/2 c. butter, melted
1/2 c. shredded Cheddar cheese
1/2 t. paprika
6 slices bacon, crisply cooked and
   crumbled

In a saucepan over medium heat, cook squash and onion in water until tender; drain and mash. Combine squash mixture, sour cream and seasonings. Pour into a greased 13"x9" baking pan. Toss together bread crumbs, butter, cheese and paprika; sprinkle over squash mixture. Top with bacon. Bake, uncovered, at 300 degrees for 20 minutes, or until hot and golden. Serves 6 to 8.

Roasted cherry tomatoes make a delightful garnish. Place tomatoes (still on the stem, if you like) in a shallow pan and drizzle with olive oil. Bake at 450 degrees for 15 minutes, or until soft and slightly wrinkled. Serve warm or chilled.

Baked Stuffed Tomatoes

Rumbledethumps

## Rumbledethumps

*A funny name for a hearty, satisfying side! Garnish with some crispy bacon to make it even better.*

1 lb. potatoes, peeled and diced
2 T. butter, sliced
1 onion, thinly sliced
2 c. cabbage, finely shredded
salt and pepper to taste

2/3 c. shredded Cheddar cheese, divided
Optional: additional butter, snipped fresh chives

Cover potatoes with water in a saucepan; bring to a boil. Reduce heat; cover and simmer for 8 minutes, or until just tender. Drain and rinse under cold water; drain again. Transfer potatoes to a bowl; mash coarsely with a fork and set aside. Meanwhile, melt butter in a skillet over low heat. Add onion and cook for 10 minutes, or until soft. Add cabbage to skillet; cook for 5 minutes. Stir in potatoes, salt and pepper. Remove from heat; stir in 2 tablespoons cheese. Transfer to a greased 13"x9" baking pan; sprinkle with remaining cheese. Bake, uncovered, at 350 degrees for 20 minutes, or until heated through. Serves 4 to 6.

133

Clean baked-on food from a baking pan...no elbow grease required! Place a dryer sheet in the pan and fill with warm water. Let it stand overnight, then sponge clean. You'll find the fabric softeners will really soften the baked-on food!

## Icebox Mashed Potatoes

*These potatoes are delicious with gravy, but really don't need any topping because they are so creamy and good! A wonderful make-ahead dish that travels well too.*

5 lbs. baking potatoes, peeled and halved
2 cubes chicken bouillon
1/2 t. garlic salt
2 t. onion powder
2 t. salt
1/4 t. pepper
16-oz. container low-fat sour cream
8-oz. pkg. reduced-fat cream cheese
2 T. butter, sliced
Optional: additional butter, snipped fresh chives

Cover potatoes with water in a deep stockpot; add bouillon and garlic salt. Bring to a boil over high heat; cook until potatoes are tender, about 20 minutes. Remove from heat; drain in a colander. Return potatoes to the same pot and mash. Add remaining ingredients except butter; mix well. Spoon potato mixture into a greased 13"x9" baking pan; dot with butter. Bake, uncovered, at 350 degrees for 40 minutes. If top browns too quickly, cover with aluminum foil for the last 10 minutes. To make ahead, allow unbaked potato mixture to cool slightly; cover with plastic wrap and refrigerate up to 3 days. To serve, let stand at room temperature for 30 minutes; uncover and bake as directed. Garnish as desired. Makes 10 to 12 servings.

Icebox Mashed Potatoes

Hawaiian Baked Beans

## Hawaiian Baked Beans

*Pineapple, baked beans and brown sugar...yum! If you're not feeding a crowd, it's simple to halve this recipe and bake it in an 8"x8" pan.*

1-3/4 c. pineapple juice
1 c. catsup
1/2 c. mustard
1-1/2 c. dark brown sugar, packed

15-oz. can pineapple chunks, drained
4 15-1/2 oz. cans navy beans & bacon, drained and rinsed

In a bowl, whisk together pineapple juice, catsup and mustard. Add brown sugar and mix well; stir in pineapple chunks. Add beans; mix well. Spoon into a greased 13"x9" baking pan. Bake, uncovered, at 350 degrees for 90 minutes, or until hot and bubbly. Serves 8 to 12.

## Kansas City Baked Beans

*Sweet, saucy barbecue flavor...try 'em at your next cookout.*

4 15-oz. cans baked beans
1/2 lb. bacon, crisply cooked and crumbled
1 onion, diced
1 c. dark brown sugar, packed

18-oz. bottle Kansas City-style or mesquite barbecue sauce
1 t. smoke-flavored cooking sauce
1/2 t. pepper

Place all ingredients in a lightly greased 13"x9" aluminum foil baking pan; stir until combined. Cover tightly with aluminum foil. Preheat a grill to medium-low. Place pan on grill for 20 minutes, stirring every 5 minutes to prevent scorching. Remove foil and grill another 5 to 10 minutes, until thickened. May also be baked in the oven at 400 degrees for 30 minutes; no need to stir. Uncover and bake another 5 to 10 minutes, until thickened. Serves 8 to 10.

If canned beans don't agree with you, just drain and rinse them well before using...you'll be washing away any "tinny" taste too.

## Texas Hominy

*Serve up a deliciously different side dish with barbecued or grilled meats.*

6 slices bacon, diced
1 onion, finely diced
1 jalapeño pepper, minced
2 cloves garlic, minced
4  15-1/2 oz. cans hominy, drained
salt and pepper to taste

1-1/2 c. shredded Cheddar cheese, divided
1-1/2 c. shredded Monterey Jack cheese, divided
1/2 c. green onions, chopped

In a skillet over medium heat, cook bacon until crisp. Remove bacon to drain on paper towels; reserve drippings in skillet. Sauté onion and jalapeño in reserved drippings until tender. Add garlic and cook one to 2 minutes longer. Stir in hominy, salt and pepper. Remove from heat; stir in one cup each of Cheddar and Monterey Jack cheeses. Spoon mixture into a greased 13"x9" baking pan. Sprinkle with remaining cheeses, bacon and onions. Bake, uncovered, at 375 degrees for 30 minutes, or until hot and bubbly. Makes 10 servings.

A western theme is fun and easy for casual get-togethers. Set the table with pie plates, Mason jar tumblers and bandanna napkins. Serve up grilled burgers and fixin's, baked beans and tortilla chips with salsa.

Texas Hominy

Best-Ever Refrigerator Rolls

## Best-Ever Refrigerator Rolls

*These rolls always turn out wonderful! This is a convenient recipe since the dough can be stirred up whenever you have a few minutes, then tucked in the fridge to bake later.*

1 c. water
2 envs. active dry yeast
1/2 c. butter, melted and slightly
   cooled
1/2 c. sugar

3 eggs, beaten
1 t. salt
4 to 4-1/2 c. all-purpose flour
Optional: additional melted butter

Heat water until very warm, about 110 to 115 degrees. In a large bowl, combine warm water and yeast. Let stand until foamy, 5 to 10 minutes. Stir in butter, sugar, eggs and salt. Beat in flour, one cup at a time, until dough is too stiff to mix. Cover with a tea towel; keep refrigerated for 2 hours to 4 days. Turn chilled dough out onto a lightly floured board. Divide dough into 24 equal pieces; roll each into a smooth ball. Place balls in even rows in a greased 13"x9" baking pan. Cover and let rise again until double, about one hour. Bake at 375 degrees for 15 to 20 minutes, until rolls are golden. Brush warm rolls with melted butter, if desired. Makes 2 dozen.

Make a fabric liner for a basket of freshly coffee cake...no sewing required! Simply use pinking shears to cut an 18-inch square of cotton fabric in a cheerful print.

## Arkansas Green Beans

*Real comfort food! Everybody is sure to go back for seconds.*

5 15-oz. cans green beans, drained
1 lb. bacon, cut into 1-inch pieces
2/3 c. brown sugar, packed
1/4 c. butter, melted
1/4 c. soy sauce
1-1/2 t. garlic powder

Place green beans in an ungreased 13"x9" baking pan; set aside. In a skillet over medium heat, cook bacon until partially done but not too crisp. Drain bacon on paper towels; set aside some bacon for topping. Scatter remaining bacon over green beans. Drizzle with a tablespoon of bacon drippings, if desired. Combine remaining ingredients in a small bowl; spoon over green bean mixture. Bake, uncovered, at 350 degrees for 40 minutes, or until heated through. Top with reserved bacon. Serves 10.

When frying bacon, prepare a few extra slices to tuck into the fridge.
Combine with juicy slices of sun-ripened tomato, frilly lettuce and
creamy mayonnaise for a fresh BLT sandwich. Tomorrow's lunch
is ready in a jiffy!

Arkansas Green Beans

Mexican Roasted Cauliflower

## Mexican Roasted Cauliflower

*A flavorful alternative to refried beans & rice that even cauliflower-haters will love.*

1/4 c. olive oil
3 cloves garlic, minced
1 T. chili powder, or to taste
1/2 t. ground cumin

1 lb. cauliflower, cut into bite-size flowerets
juice of 1 lime
1/4 c. fresh cilantro, chopped

Mix oil, garlic and spices in a large bowl. Add cauliflower; toss to coat. Spread in an ungreased shallow 13"x9" baking pan. Bake, uncovered, at 325 degrees for one hour and 15 minutes, stirring occasionally. Remove from oven. Drizzle with lime juice; sprinkle with cilantro and toss well. Serve warm. Makes 6 servings.

145

All kinds of vegetables become deliciously sweet when roasted... asparagus, carrots, squash, bell peppers and Brussels sprouts, just to name a few. Toss peeled, sliced veggies with olive oil and spread on a baking sheet. Bake at 350 degrees for about 30 minutes, stirring occasionally, until tender.

## Spicy Carrot French Fries

*Give potatoes the night off...kids will love these fries!*

2 lbs. carrots, peeled and cut into
  matchsticks
4 T. olive oil, divided
1 T. seasoned salt

2 t. ground cumin
1 t. chili powder
1 t. pepper
Garnish: ranch salad dressing

Place carrots in a plastic zipping bag. Sprinkle with 3 tablespoons oil and seasonings; toss to coat. Drizzle remaining oil in a shallow 13"x9" baking pan; arrange carrots in a single layer in pan. Bake, uncovered, at 425 degrees for 25 to 35 minutes, until carrots are golden. Serve with salad dressing for dipping. Makes 4 to 6 servings.

## Fabulous Fries

*Yum...you'll love this new way to make French fries!*

2 lbs. potatoes, peeled and cut into
  1/4-inch strips

1 to 1-1/2 c. light Italian salad
  dressing

Place potatoes in a bowl; drizzle with salad dressing and stir to coat. Transfer to a 13"x9" baking pan coated with non-stick vegetable spray. Bake, uncovered, at 325 degrees for 12 to 15 minutes; turn with a spatula. Bake an additional 10 minutes, or until crisp and golden. Makes 6 to 8 servings.

White paper coffee filters are great for serving up burgers and hot dogs...no spills, no mess and easy for little hands to hold! Afterwards, just toss them away.

Spicy Carrot French Fries

Broccoli Cornbread

## Broccoli Cornbread

*Why settle for plain cornbread? This tasty recipe will dress up any menu.*

2  8-1/2 oz. pkgs. cornbread mix
16-oz. container small-curd cottage
   cheese
2 eggs, beaten
1 onion, chopped

10-oz. pkg. frozen chopped
   broccoli, thawed and well
   drained
1/2 c. shredded Cheddar cheese

In a large bowl, combine dry cornbread mix, cottage cheese, eggs and onion; mix well. Fold in broccoli. Transfer batter to a greased 13"x9" glass baking pan. Bake, uncovered, at 350 degrees for 35 minutes, or until a toothpick comes out clean. While still warm, sprinkle with Cheddar cheese. Allow to cool; cut into squares. Makes 12 to 15 servings.

Take it easy on alternate Friday nights...arrange for a friendly dinner swap! One week, you make a double batch of a favorite casserole and deliver one to a friend. Next week, she returns the favor. You're sure to discover some great new recipes while gaining a little free time too.

## Pamela's Garlic Bread

*People will wait around the kitchen waiting for this to come out of the oven!*

8-oz. pkg. cream cheese, softened
4-oz. can chopped black olives, drained
4 green onions, chopped
2 to 3 cloves garlic, finely chopped
1 T. Italian seasoning
1/4 c. butter, softened
1 loaf French bread, halved lengthwise

In a bowl, combine all ingredients except bread; mix until well blended. Evenly spread mixture over cut sides of bread. Place bread in an ungreased shallow 13"x9" baking pan. Bake, uncovered, at 350 degrees for 10 to 15 minutes, until bubbly and golden. Cool slightly and slice. Makes 12 servings.

Roast garlic is heavenly to spread on bread and so easy in the microwave! Slice the top off a whole garlic bulb and set it in a microwave-safe dish. Sprinkle to taste with olive oil, salt and pepper. Add a little water and cover with plastic wrap. Heat on high setting for 8 minutes, or until soft.

Pamela's Garlic Bread

Cheesy Garlic Rolls

## Cheesy Garlic Rolls

*Great with lasagna or hot soup!*

2 12-ct. pkgs. frozen dinner rolls
1/2 c. butter, cubed
2 t. garlic powder

1/2 c. grated Parmesan cheese, divided

Place frozen rolls in a greased 13"x9" baking pan; set aside. Microwave butter in a microwave-safe bowl until melted; stir in garlic powder. Brush butter mixture over rolls; sprinkle with 1/4 cup cheese. Let rolls rise according to package instructions. Bake at 350 degrees for 15 to 20 minutes, until golden. Brush with any remaining butter mixture and sprinkle with remaining cheese. Makes 2 dozen rolls.

A single vintage quilt patch makes a cozy topper for a bread basket...just stitch it to a large napkin in a matching color.

## Roasted Veggies & Penne Pasta

*This recipe is great for getting everyone to eat more vegetables!*

16-oz. pkg. penne pasta, uncooked
2 zucchini, quartered lengthwise
  and sliced 1-inch thick
2 yellow squash, quartered
  lengthwise and sliced 1-inch
  thick
2 red peppers, cut into 1-inch
  squares
1 onion, cut into 1-inch squares
1 to 2 T. olive oil
kosher salt to taste
3 c. shredded mozzarella cheese,
  divided
1/4 c. plus 2 T. grated Parmesan
  cheese, divided

Cook pasta according to package directions, just until tender; drain. Meanwhile, combine vegetables in a greased 13"x9" baking pan. Drizzle with oil and season with salt. Bake, uncovered, at 425 degrees for 15 to 20 minutes, stirring once or twice, until golden and caramelized. Add cooked pasta to vegetable mixture along with 2 cups mozzarella cheese and 1/4 cup Parmesan cheese. Toss to mix well. Sprinkle with remaining cheeses. Return to oven for 5 minutes, or until cheese melts. Makes 6 to 8 servings.

154

## Crunchy Veggie Bake

*This casserole with its crunchy topping is always a hit!*

3 16-oz. pkgs. frozen broccoli,
  carrot and cauliflower blend,
  thawed
2 10-3/4 oz. cans cream of
  mushroom soup
1 c. mayonnaise
1 T. garlic powder
1/4 t. pepper
8-oz. pkg. shredded Cheddar
  cheese
6-oz. can French fried onions

Spread vegetables in a greased 13"x9" baking pan. In a bowl, combine soup, mayonnaise and seasonings; mix well. Stir in cheese and set aside. Spoon soup mixture over veggies; toss evenly to coat. Bake, uncovered, at 350 degrees for 35 to 40 minutes. Sprinkle with onions. Bake an additional 5 minutes, or until onions are golden. Makes 10 to 12 servings.

Roasted Veggies & Penne Pasta

Luke's Tortellini Salad

# Toss-Together Sides

## Luke's Tortellini Salad

*This pasta salad is easy, delicious and colorful.*

16-oz. pkg. refrigerated cheese
   tortellini, uncooked
2 green peppers, chopped
2 c. cherry tomatoes, halved

6-oz. can sliced black olives,
   drained
light Italian salad dressing to taste
1 c. grated Parmesan cheese

Cook tortellini according to package directions; drain and rinse with cold water. Transfer tortellini to a 13"x9" glass baking pan; refrigerate until cooled. Mix in peppers, tomatoes and olives. Just before serving time, stir in salad dressing and cheese. Serves 4.

## Bell Pepper Slaw

*This colorful slaw's flavor is best when made a day before serving... convenient for potlucks!*

10-oz. pkg. angel hair shredded
   coleslaw
5 assorted peppers (green, red,
   orange, yellow and/or purple),
   thinly sliced
1 c. red and/or yellow cherry
   tomatoes, halved

3/4 c. zesty Italian salad dressing
1/4 c. sweet balsamic salad
   dressing
1 T. sugar
1 t. dried basil
1 t. dried oregano
1 t. kosher salt

Combine coleslaw, peppers and tomatoes in a 13"x9" glass baking pan. Stir and set aside. In a small bowl, combine remaining ingredients. Whisk well and pour over coleslaw mixture; toss to coat. For best flavor, cover and refrigerate overnight. Makes 12 servings.

Spoon servings of salad or slaw into hollowed-out tomato halves... so pretty on the dining table!

## 11-Layer Garden in a Bowl

*This farm-fresh salad is for those occasions when seven layers just won't do!*

3 c. mayonnaise
2/3 c. sugar
2  10-oz. pkgs. mixed salad greens, divided
1 lb. bacon, crisply cooked and crumbled
1 red onion, diced
10-oz. pkg. frozen peas, thawed
1 green pepper, diced
2 c. cauliflower flowerets
2 c. broccoli flowerets
1 c. sliced mushrooms
1 c. shredded Cheddar cheese
1 c. cherry tomatoes, halved
1 T. Italian seasoning

In a bowl, mix mayonnaise and sugar until blended; set aside. Layer half the salad greens in an 13"x9" glass baking pan. Layer with half the mayonnaise mixture, and half of each remaining ingredient except tomatoes and seasoning. Repeat layers. Top with tomatoes and sprinkle with seasoning. Cover and refrigerate 2 hours before serving. Makes 8 servings.

Lacy cheese crisps are tasty with salads. Spoon mounds of freshly shredded Parmesan cheese, 4 inches apart, onto a baking sheet lined with parchment paper. Bake at 400 degrees for 5 to 7 minutes, until melted and golden, then cool.

11-Layer Garden in a Bowl

Minty Melon Salad

## Minty Melon Salad

*Fresh mint really brings out the sweetness of the juicy melon
in this bright and summery salad.*

1 c. water
3/4 c. sugar
3 T. lime juice
2 t. fresh mint, chopped
5 c. watermelon, cubed

3 c. cantaloupe, cubed
3 c. honeydew, cubed
2 c. nectarines, pitted and sliced
1 c. blueberries
Garnish: fresh mint sprigs

Combine water, sugar, juice and mint in a saucepan; bring to a boil. Boil
for 2 minutes, stirring constantly. Remove from heat; cover and cool
completely. Meanwhile, combine fruit in a 13"x9" glass baking pan. Pour
cooled dressing over fruit; stir until well coated. Cover and chill for at least
2 hours, stirring occasionally. Drain liquid before serving. Garnish with
fresh mint sprigs. Serves 10 to 12.

161

Here's a simple way to peel a melon! Slice off both ends, then stand the
melon on one cut end. With a flexible knife, slice down to remove the
peel in strips. Cut the melon in half, scoop out the seeds with a spoon
and cut the melon into cubes.

## Warm Orzo Salad

*Most of the ingredients for this colorful dish can be kept in the pantry... so convenient when you've just remembered this evening's potluck!*

16-oz. pkg. orzo pasta, uncooked
12-oz. jar roasted red peppers, drained and large pieces cut up
6-oz. can black olives, drained and halved
14-oz. jar artichoke hearts, drained
3-1/2 oz. jar capers, drained
1 c. pine nuts
Garnish: cherry tomatoes, additional pine nuts

Cook orzo according to package directions. Drain; transfer orzo to a 13"x9" glass baking pan. Mix in remaining ingredients. Toss with desired amount of Olive Oil Dressing. Serve warm. Serves 10 to 15.

### Olive Oil Dressing:

1/2 to 3/4 c. olive oil
juice of 1/2 lemon
2 T. garlic, minced
1 T. fresh oregano, chopped, or to taste
2 t. fresh parsley, chopped

Make dressing ahead of time by shaking all ingredients together in a covered jar. Cover and chill before using.

For hearty salads in a snap, keep unopened cans of diced tomatoes, black olives, garbanzo beans and marinated artichokes in the fridge. They'll be chilled and ready to toss with fresh greens at a moment's notice.

Warm Orzo Salad

Noodle Kugel

## Noodle Kugel

*A sweet noodle dish that goes well with baked ham...*
*it can double as a dessert too.*

16-oz. pkg. wide egg noodles,
   uncooked
3/4 to 1 c. butter, melted
16-oz. container sour cream
20-oz. can crushed pineapple,
   drained

4 eggs, beaten
1 c. sugar
1/2 t. salt
2 t. vanilla extract
Optional: cinnamon

Cook noodles according to package directions; drain. Combine noodles and remaining ingredients in a greased 13"x9" baking pan. Bake, uncovered, at 350 degrees for one hour, or until heated through. Top with a sprinkle of cinnamon, if using. Serves 10 to 12.

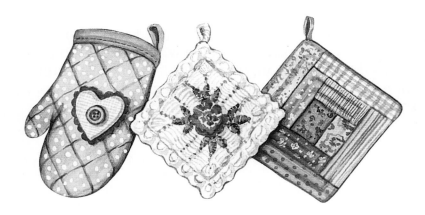

Platters of food set on different levels make a more interesting presentation. Use a stack of plates or upside-down pots and bowls on a buffet table to create different heights. Simply cover with a tablecloth and set serving dishes on top.

Two for one! Double a favorite side dish and freeze half. Another night, turn the remaining portion into a main dish by adding some meat to it. Salsa rice with cubed chicken, baked beans with sliced sausage and macaroni & cheese with diced ham are just a few tasty ideas.

Baking more than one pan at a time? Remember to stagger them on the oven racks so the food will cook evenly.

Free up your favorite baking pan when putting a made-ahead recipe in the freezer. Line the pan with aluminum foil, add recipe ingredients, wrap and freeze...lift out the frozen casserole and return to the freezer. To serve, slip it back into the same pan and bake.

If time is short, keep side dishes simple and quick to fix... thick slices of tomatoes layered with mozzarella cheese and drizzled with olive oil, new potatoes boiled just until tender, then tossed with butter and parsley, or big bowls of fresh fruit all are simple and delicious.

# Parties
# in a Pan

## Baked Artichoke Squares

*Party-perfect...these scrumptious little morsels are sure to go quickly!*

2 6-oz. jars marinated artichoke
  hearts
1/2 c. onion, chopped
1 clove garlic, minced
4 eggs, beaten

1/4 c. dry bread crumbs
1/2 t. fresh Italian parsley, chopped
2 c. shredded Cheddar cheese
salt and pepper to taste

Drain liquid from one jar of artichokes into a skillet; drain liquid from remaining jar and discard. Chop all artichokes and set aside. Heat liquid in skillet over medium heat. Sauté onion and garlic until soft; drain. In a bowl, combine eggs, bread crumbs and parsley. Stir in onion mixture, chopped artichokes, cheese, salt and pepper. Pour mixture into a greased 13"x9" baking pan. Bake at 325 degrees for 30 to 35 minutes. Cool; cut into small squares. Serves 8 to 10.

## Cheesy Artichoke Dip

*The best artichoke dip you'll ever taste! Delicious and so fast to put together.*

16-oz. pkg. shredded Parmesan
  cheese
8-oz. pkg. shredded mozzarella
  cheese
1 c. mayonnaise

2 c. canned artichoke hearts,
  drained and chopped
1 t. garlic, minced
pita chips or sliced French bread

In a large bowl, mix together all ingredients except pita chips or bread. Spread in a greased 13"x9" baking pan. Bake, uncovered, at 350 degrees for 20 to 30 minutes, until bubbly and edges are lightly golden. Serve with pita chips or bread. Makes 12 to 15 servings.

For stand-up parties, make it easy on guests by serving foods that can be eaten in just one or 2 bites.

Baked Artichoke Squares

Barbecue Drummies

# Parties in a Pan

## Barbecue Drummies

*Love saucy chicken wings? Drumsticks are meatier and less messy than wings! Pack the baking pan of drummies in a portable carrier to take to picnics and sporting events.*

14-oz. can whole-berry cranberry
  sauce
12-oz. bottle chili sauce
2 T. red pepper flakes

3 lbs. chicken drumsticks
2 T. olive oil
Garnish: ranch or blue cheese salad
  dressing, celery sticks

Combine cranberry sauce, chili sauce and red pepper flakes in a one-gallon plastic zipping bag. Knead bag to mix. Remove 1/2 cup of sauce mixture and refrigerate. Pat drumsticks dry with a paper towel; add to bag. Seal bag and refrigerate for at least one hour. Remove drumsticks to a greased 13"x9" glass baking pan, discarding sauce mixture in bag. Bake, uncovered, at 375 degrees for about 25 minutes. Turn drumsticks over; baste with reserved sauce mixture. Bake for another 7 to 10 minutes, until chicken juices run clear when pierced. Serve drumsticks with salad dressing and celery sticks for dipping. Makes 8 to 12 servings.

## West Texas Party Drumsticks

*A crunchy alternative to traditional chicken wings.*

1 c. ranch salad dressing
1 T. hot pepper sauce
1 c. corn flake cereal crumbs

1-1/4 oz. pkg. taco seasoning mix
12 chicken drumsticks

In a shallow dish, combine salad dressing and hot sauce. In a separate dish or a plastic zipping bag, combine crumbs and taco seasoning. Dip drumsticks in salad dressing mixture; coat well with crumb mixture. Arrange in a greased 13"x9" baking pan. Bake, uncovered, at 350 degrees for one hour, or until juices run clear. Serves 4 to 6.

Serving sticky finger foods like chicken wings? Set out a basket of washcloths, moistened with lemon-scented water and warmed briefly in the microwave. Guests will thank you!

## Gingered Coconut Chicken Fingers

*Sure to be a hit at get-togethers!*

3/4 c. sweetened flaked coconut
3 T. plain dry bread crumbs
3/4 t. ground ginger
1/2 t. cayenne pepper
2 T. honey

1 t. lemon or orange juice
14-oz. pkg. chicken tenders, sliced
   in half crosswise
salt to taste

In a blender or food processor, combine coconut, bread crumbs and spices. Pulse to blend; transfer to a shallow dish. Blend honey and juice in a separate shallow dish. Season chicken pieces with salt; coat in honey mixture and roll in coconut mixture. Arrange chicken in a lightly greased 13"x9" baking pan. Bake at 400 degrees for 12 to 15 minutes, until chicken is tender and no longer pink. Serve with Sour Cream Sauce. Makes about one dozen.

### Sour Cream Sauce:

1/3 c. sour cream
2 T. crushed pineapple with juice

1/4 t. ground ginger

Mix well; chill until serving time.

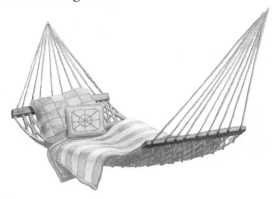

Light and fizzy...a perfect party drink! Combine 6 cups chilled pineapple juice, one cup lime juice and one cup sugar. Stir in 2 liters sparkling water and serve over crushed ice.

Gingered Coconut Chicken Fingers

Ham & Swiss Cheese Rolls

## Ham & Swiss Cheese Rolls

*An all-time favorite party recipe...you just can't go wrong with a tray of these buttery little sandwiches!*

3/4 c. butter
1-1/2 T. Worcestershire sauce
1/2 t. dry mustard
1-1/2 t. poppy seed

2 t. dried, minced onion
2 12-ct. pkgs. Hawaiian rolls
1 lb. thinly sliced deli ham
1/2 lb. sliced Swiss cheese

Combine butter, Worcestershire sauce, mustard, poppy seed and onion in a small saucepan. Bring to a boil over medium heat; remove from heat. Slice individual rolls in half. Make sandwiches using bread, ham and cheese; arrange in an ungreased 13"x9" baking pan. Spoon butter mixture over sandwiches. Bake, uncovered, at 350 degrees for 15 minutes. Makes 2 dozen.

If the weather is sunny and warm, why not enjoy dinner outdoors? Just toss a red-checked tablecloth on the backyard picnic table and serve sandwiches on paper plates with a big pitcher of sweet tea. Enjoy!

## Antipasto Kabobs

*Easy-to-pick-up party food! Add some crunchy bread sticks for
a light warm-weather meal.*

1/3 c. olive oil
1/3 c. balsamic vinegar
1 T. fresh thyme, minced
1 clove garlic, minced
1 t. sugar
9-oz. pkg. cheese-filled tortellini,
  cooked
5-oz. pkg. thinly sliced salami

12-oz. jar artichoke hearts, drained
  and quartered
5-3/4 oz. jar green olives with
  pimentos, drained
16-oz. jar banana peppers, drained
1 pt. cherry tomatoes
16 6-inch skewers, soaked in
  water

Whisk together oil, vinegar, thyme, garlic and sugar in a small bowl; set
aside. Thread remaining ingredients onto skewers alternately in order given.
Arrange skewers in a single layer in a 13"x9" glass baking pan; drizzle with
marinade. Cover and refrigerate for 2 to 3 hours, turning occasionally. Drain
and discard marinade before serving. Makes 16 servings.

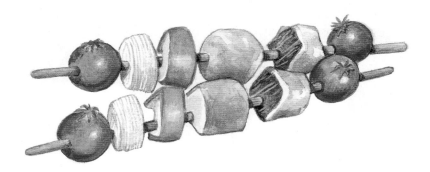

The olive oil marinade for the Antipasto Kabobs makes a delicious
salad dressing too...why not make a double batch?

Antipasto Kabobs

Monterey Mushroom Squares

# Parties in a Pan

## Monterey Mushroom Squares

*These cheesy squares are irresistible! Mix & match different kinds of mushrooms and cheeses for variety.*

8-oz. tube refrigerated crescent
  rolls
2 c. sliced mushrooms
1/4 c. butter, melted

1/2 c. shredded Monterey Jack
  cheese
1/2 t. dried oregano
1/4 t. onion salt

Separate dough into 2 long rectangles. Press into the bottom and 1/2-inch up the sides of a lightly greased 13"x9" baking pan. Toss mushrooms with melted butter; spoon over dough. Sprinkle with remaining ingredients. Bake, uncovered, at 375 degrees for 20 to 25 minutes. Cut into squares; serve warm. Makes 2 dozen.

## Mini Stuffed Peppers

*Delicious bites of sausage and cream cheese...these won't last very long!*

1 lb. mini sweet peppers, halved
  and seeds removed
1 lb. ground pork sausage,
  browned and drained

1-1/2 c. cream cheese, softened
1/2 t. garlic powder
1/2 t. onion powder

Add peppers to a saucepan of boiling water. Boil for 4 minutes; drain on paper towels. Combine remaining ingredients in a bowl. Spoon mixture into pepper halves, filling 1/2 full. Place on an ungreased shallow 13"x9" baking pan. Bake at 375 degrees for 15 minutes, until golden and peppers are fork-tender. Makes about 4 dozen.

*It's a lovely thing...everyone sitting down together, sharing food.*
*-Alice May Brock*

# Parties in a Pan

## Bake & Share BBQ Meatballs

*A wonderful recipe to share with friends! Bake a pan for your family and share a second pan with friends. Or enjoy now and tuck a pan in your freezer for later.*

3 lbs. lean ground beef or turkey
1 c. evaporated milk
2 c. quick-cooking oats, uncooked
2 eggs, beaten

1 onion, chopped
2 t. chili powder
1/2 t. garlic salt
1/2 t. pepper

Combine all ingredients in a large bowl; mix well. Form into 2-inch balls, by hand or using a small scoop. Place meatballs in a single layer in 2 ungreased 13"x9" baking pans. If desired, cover and refrigerate up to one day, or wrap well and freeze unbaked. Spoon warm BBQ Sauce over meatballs, thawed if frozen. Cover and bake at 350 degrees for one hour, or until bubbly and meatballs are no longer pink in the center. Makes 24 servings.

## BBQ Sauce:

2 c. catsup
1-1/2 c. brown sugar, packed
1/2 c. onion, chopped

2 T. smoke-flavored cooking sauce
1/2 t. garlic powder

Combine all ingredients; mix well. Microwave or simmer in a saucepan until heated through and brown sugar is dissolved.

Making lots of meatballs? Grab a melon baller and start scooping... you'll be done in record time!

Bake & Share BBQ Meatballs

Deluxe Cocktail Sausages

## Deluxe Cocktail Sausages

*A deliciously sweet and savory appetizer...*
*a perfect start to any get-together!*

1/2 c. butter
3 T. brown sugar, packed
3 T. honey
1/2 c. chopped pecans

8-oz. tube refrigerated crescent
   rolls, separated
24 mini smoked cocktail sausages

Preheat oven to 400 degrees. As oven is warming, melt butter in oven in a 13"x9" glass baking pan. Add brown sugar, honey and pecans to melted butter; stir to coat bottom of the pan and set aside. Slice each crescent roll triangle into thirds. Roll each smaller triangle around one sausage. Place on butter mixture, seam-side down. Bake, uncovered, at 400 degrees for 15 minutes, or until golden. Makes 2 dozen.

Just for fun, pick up a stack of retro-style plastic burger baskets. Lined with colorful paper napkins, they'll be easy for guests to fill with party foods. Clean-up is a snap too...just toss away the napkins.

## Buffalo Potato Wedges

*Wonderful as either an appetizer or a side dish.*

6 to 8 potatoes, sliced into wedges
1 to 2 T. olive oil
salt, pepper and garlic powder
   to taste

1/4 c. butter, melted
1/2 c. hot pepper sauce
Optional: blue cheese salad
   dressing

Arrange potato wedges in a 13"x9" baking pan coated with non-stick vegetable spray. Drizzle with olive oil; sprinkle with seasonings. Bake at 375 degrees for about 30 minutes, until tender, tossing occasionally. Remove pan from oven. Combine butter and hot sauce in a microwave-safe cup. Microwave on high until butter is melted; stir to combine. Drizzle butter mixture over potato wedges; bake for an additional 15 minutes. Serve potato wedges with salad dressing for dipping, if desired. Makes 6 to 8 servings.

## Bacon Delights

*An appetizer for all you bacon-lovers out there.*
*Better save one for yourself!*

1/2 c. catsup
1/4 c. brown sugar, packed
1/4 c. steak sauce
2 t. Worcestershire sauce

2 T. water
8-oz. can sliced water chestnuts,
   drained
1 lb. thin-sliced bacon, halved

In a saucepan over medium-low heat, combine catsup, brown sugar and sauces. Simmer, stirring often, until brown sugar is dissolved. Remove from heat; stir in water and set aside. Place one slice water chestnut on each half-slice of bacon and roll up; secure with a wooden toothpick. Arrange in a well-greased 13"x9" baking pan; spoon warm sauce over all. Bake, uncovered, at 400 degrees for 12 to 15 minutes, until bacon is crisp and sauce is gooey. Best served at room temperature. Serves 8 to 10.

A relish tray of crisp bite-size vegetables like baby carrots, cherry tomatoes, broccoli flowerets and celery stalks is always welcome.

Buffalo Potato Wedges

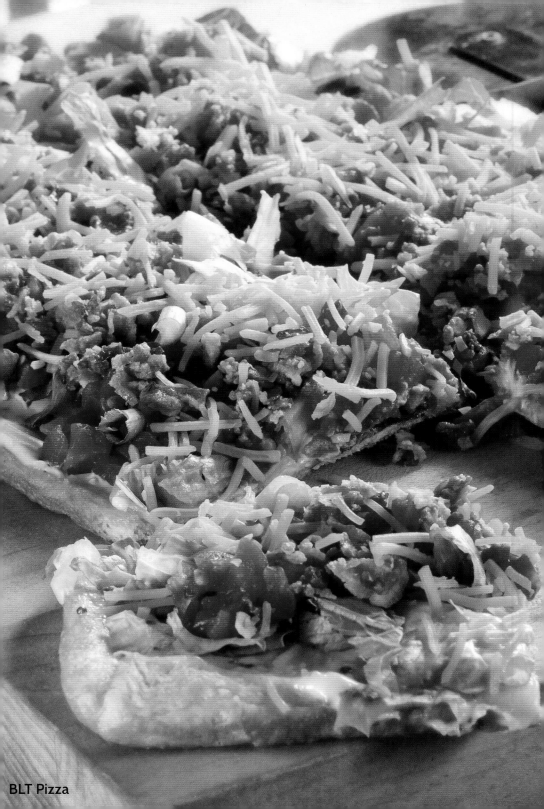

BLT Pizza

## BLT Pizza

*If you like BLT sandwiches, you will love this tasty cool appetizer pizza.*

8-oz. tube refrigerated crescent rolls
3/4 c. mayonnaise
1 T. Dijon mustard
9 slices bacon, crisply cooked and crumbled

8-oz. pkg. shredded Cheddar cheese
2 green onions, finely chopped
2 to 3 c. lettuce, shredded
3 roma tomatoes, seeded and chopped

Roll out crescent rolls in a lightly greased 13"x9" baking pan, pinching seams to seal. Bake at 375 degrees for 12 to 15 minutes, until lightly golden. Remove from oven; cool. In a small bowl, combine mayonnaise and mustard; spread over crescent rolls. Top with remaining ingredients. Cut into squares. Serves 10 to 12.

Do you have lots of kids coming over for an after-game party? Make it easy with do-it-yourself tacos or mini pizzas...guests can add their own favorite toppings. Round out the menu with pitchers of soft drinks and a delicious dessert. Simple and fun!

## Herby Bubble Bread

*Perfect to take to a potluck or serve with soup. If you're looking for extra oomph, shake in some red pepper flakes!*

3  1-lb. loaves frozen bread dough,
   thawed but still chilled
1/4 c. olive oil
3 T. Italian salad dressing mix

1 c. shredded sharp Cheddar cheese
1 t. garlic, minced
1 red onion, finely chopped

Cut dough into one-inch cubes; place in a large bowl. Pour remaining ingredients over top. Using your hands, toss until dough cubes are coated. Transfer dough cubes to a greased 13"x9" baking pan. Place in a warm area; cover and let rise until double in size. Bake at 350 degrees for 20 to 25 minutes, until golden. Serves 6 to 8.

Mix up your own Italian seasoning for pasta dishes, soups, salad and garlic bread. A good basic blend is 2 tablespoons each of dried oregano, thyme, basil, marjoram and rosemary...add or subtract to suit your family's taste. Store in a big shaker jar.

Herby Bubble Bread

Jalapeño Cheese Squares

## Jalapeño Cheese Squares

*Increase or decrease the jalapeño peppers to your preference.*

2 c. shredded Cheddar cheese
2 c. shredded Monterey Jack cheese
3/4 c. pickled jalapeño pepper
   slices, drained

2 eggs, beaten
1/2 c. all-purpose flour
12-oz. can evaporated milk

Mix together cheeses in a large bowl; spread half of mixture in a greased 13"x9" baking pan. Top with peppers; sprinkle remaining cheese mixture over top. In a bowl, stir together eggs, flour and evaporated milk. Pour batter over cheese mixture. Bake, uncovered, at 350 degrees for 25 to 30 minutes, until set and cheese is melted. Let cool slightly; cut into squares. Serves 4 to 6.

## Jalapeño Popper Dip

*This spicy dip tastes just like your favorite Mexican restaurant appetizer.*

191

2 8-oz. pkgs. cream cheese,
   softened
1 c. mayonnaise
4-oz. can sliced jalapeño peppers,
   drained and diced

4-oz. can diced green chiles
1/4 c. shredded Cheddar cheese
1/2 c. shredded Parmesan cheese
1/4 c. dry bread crumbs
assorted crackers or chips

In a bowl, mix together all ingredients except Parmesan cheese, bread crumbs and crackers or chips. Spoon mixture into an ungreased 13"x9" baking pan. Sprinkle Parmesan cheese and bread crumbs over top. Bake, uncovered, at 350 degrees for 25 to 30 minutes, until bubbly and golden. Serve warm with crackers and chips. Serves 20 to 25.

A 250-degree oven keeps hot appetizers toasty until you're ready
to serve them.

## Hot & Melty Taco Dip

*Get the party started with this panful of sassy, cheesy goodness!*

16-oz. can refried beans
1-1/2 oz. pkg. taco seasoning mix
16-oz. container sour cream
8-oz. pkg. cream cheese, softened
16-oz. jar salsa
8-oz. pkg. shredded sharp Cheddar
  cheese

Garnish: shredded lettuce, chopped
  tomatoes, sliced black olives,
  jalapeño peppers, green onions
scoop-type tortilla chips

In a bowl, combine refried beans with taco seasoning. Spread in the bottom of a lightly greased 13"x9" glass baking pan; set aside. In a separate bowl, blend sour cream and cream cheese; spread over bean layer. Spoon salsa over sour cream layer; sprinkle cheese on top. Bake, uncovered, at 350 degrees for about 25 minutes, until beans are warmed through and cheese is melted. Garnish with desired toppings. Serve with tortilla chips. Makes 8 servings.

Mix up some salsa in a jiffy! Pour a 15-ounce can of stewed tomatoes, several slices of canned jalapeños and a teaspoon or 2 of the jalapeño juice into a blender. Cover and process to the desired consistency.

Hot & Melty Taco Dip

Greek 7-Layer Dip

## Greek 7-Layer Dip

*Looking for something different on game days? This cool taste of the Mediterranean will score a touchdown with everyone!*

8-oz. container chive & onion cream cheese spread
8-oz. container hummus
1 cucumber, peeled and chopped
3 to 4 roma tomatoes, chopped
2-1/4 oz. can sliced black olives, drained
4-oz. container crumbled feta cheese
4 green onions, chopped
pita chips or white corn tortilla chips

Spread cream cheese spread evenly in the bottom of a 13"x9" glass baking pan. Drop hummus over cream cheese by small spoonfuls; spread evenly. Top with remaining ingredients except chips in order listed. Serve with pita or tortilla chips. Makes 15 servings.

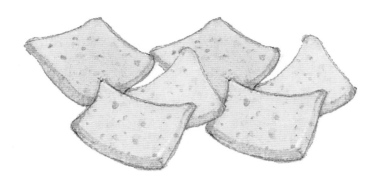

Make your own crunchy pita chips for dipping. Cut pita bread rounds into triangles, brush lightly with olive oil and sprinkle with garlic salt or herbs. Bake at 350 degrees for a few minutes, until crisp.

## Cincinnati-Style Chili Dip

*In Cincinnati, it's just not a tailgate party unless this warm dip is being passed around. Try to find a chili with cinnamon for an authentic Queen City experience!*

2 8-oz. pkgs. cream cheese, softened
2 10-1/2 oz. cans Cincinnati-style or plain chili without beans
16-oz. pkg. shredded mild Cheddar cheese
tortilla chips

Spread cream cheese in an ungreased 13"x9" glass baking pan. Pour chili over top and sprinkle with cheese. Bake, uncovered, at 350 degrees for 15 to 20 minutes, until cheese is melted. Serve with tortilla chips. Makes 10 servings.

A large unfolded map makes a clever party table topper! Sure to spark conversations about places you've been and spots you'd like to visit.

Cincinnati-Style Chili Dip

Sticky Honey Chicken Wings

# Parties in a Pan

## Sticky Honey Chicken Wings

*You'll want plenty of napkins for these tasty wings! Like it hot? Just add a shake of hot pepper sauce.*

2-1/2 lbs. chicken wings, separated
salt and pepper to taste
1/2 c. honey
1/2 c. soy sauce
2 T. catsup
1/2 t. garlic powder
1/2 t. ground ginger

Line a shallow 13"x9" baking pan with heavy-duty aluminum foil; coat with non-stick vegetable spray and set aside. Lightly season chicken wings on all sides with salt and pepper. Arrange chicken wings in pan. Bake at 425 degrees for 20 minutes. Meanwhile, whisk together remaining ingredients in a bowl. Remove wings from oven; drain. Spoon or brush sauce over wings. Return to oven for another 20 to 25 minutes, turning wings over in sauce every 5 minutes, until well glazed and chicken juices run clear. Makes about 10 servings.

## Spicy BBQ Chicken Wings

*These wings are easy to make, bake and take...irresistible too.*

2-1/2 lbs. chicken wings, separated
1 c. barbecue sauce
1/4 c. hot pepper sauce

Place wings in a lightly greased 13"x9" baking pan. Bake, uncovered, at 400 degrees for 20 minutes. Remove wings from oven; drain. Turn wings over; bake for another 20 minutes. Meanwhile, combine sauces in a bowl. Add sauce to wings; stir until evenly coated. Bake, uncovered, for another 30 minutes, or until wings are cooked through and sauce is thickened. Serves 6 to 8.

Boneless chicken tenders can be substituted in most baked chicken wing recipes. Thread them onto wooden skewers for serving ease, and watch closely as they bake...they'll be done in less time than wings.

## Mushroom Poppers

*It's the best of both worlds...a stuffed mushroom and a jalapeño popper in one tasty bite!*

16 mushrooms
2 cloves garlic, minced
2 jalapeño peppers, finely chopped, ribs and seeds removed
1 T. olive oil
6 T. shredded Cheddar cheese

2 3-oz. pkgs. cream cheese, softened
4 slices bacon, crisply cooked and crumbled
salt and pepper to taste

Separate mushroom stems from caps. Set caps aside; finely chop stems. In a skillet over medium heat, combine chopped stems, garlic, peppers and oil. Cook and stir until mushrooms are tender, about 10 minutes. Transfer mushroom mixture to a bowl; stir in cheeses and bacon. Season with salt and pepper. Spoon mushroom mixture generously into reserved mushroom caps; arrange caps in a lightly greased 13"x9" baking pan. Bake, uncovered, at 350 degrees for 15 to 20 minutes, until golden on top. Makes 16.

200

## Hi Hat Mushrooms

*These savory stuffed mushrooms are sure to be a hit at any gathering.*

1 lb. whole mushrooms
1 lb. ground pork sausage
8-oz. can tomato sauce
1 c. white wine or chicken broth

1/2 clove garlic, minced and mashed
1/8 t. dried oregano

Remove and chop mushroom stems; mix stems into sausage. Stuff mushroom caps with mixture, rounding into high crowns or "hats." Arrange in an ungreased 13"x9" baking pan. Bake, uncovered, at 350 degrees for 30 minutes. Meanwhile, mix remaining ingredients in a saucepan; simmer over medium-low heat. When mushrooms are done baking, add them to sauce. Cover and simmer over low heat for 15 minutes. Serves 8.

Mushroom Poppers

Pepper Poppers

## Pepper Poppers

*So yummy...these will be a hit at any gathering! Easily made ahead of party time too...simply cover with aluminum foil and refrigerate, then bake to serve hot.*

1 lb. bacon, crisply cooked and
   crumbled
1-1/2 c. cream cheese, softened
1/4 t. garlic powder
1/4 t. salt
12 jalapeño peppers, halved and
   seeds removed

1 c. shredded Cheddar or Monterey
   Jack cheese
1/2 to 1 c. dry bread crumbs
Optional: ranch salad dressing or
   sour cream

In a large skillet over medium heat, cook bacon until crisp; drain well and crumble. Meanwhile, add cream cheese to a large bowl. Blend in seasonings; add crumbled bacon and mix well. Spoon 2 tablespoons cheese mixture into each pepper half. If any cheese mixture is left, divide among peppers. Put bread crumbs in a shallow dish. Roll peppers in bread crumbs; place in a lightly greased 13"x9" baking pan. Bake, uncovered, at 350 degrees for 30 to 35 minutes, until bubbly and golden. Serve with salad dressing or sour cream, if desired. Makes 2 dozen.

203

When making any dish with hot jalapeño peppers, be sure to to wear plastic gloves to avoid irritation while cutting, slicing and chopping. Don't touch your face, lips or eyes while you're working! Just toss away the gloves when you're done.

## Pepperoni Squares

*Company coming and you need a quick appetizer? This will give your guests a warm welcome!*

2 c. milk
2 eggs, beaten
1-1/2 c. all-purpose flour
1 lb. Muenster cheese, diced
8-oz. pkg. pepperoni, chopped

1/2 t. dried oregano
1/4 t. dried parsley
1/4 t. pepper
1 c. shredded pizza-blend cheese
Garnish: warmed pizza sauce

Combine milk, eggs, flour, Muenster cheese, pepperoni and spices in a large bowl. Mix well; pour into a lightly greased 13"x9" baking pan. Bake at 350 degrees for 25 minutes. Remove from oven; sprinkle with pizza-blend cheese. Bake for an additional 5 to 8 minutes, until melted. Cool slightly; cut into squares. Serve with pizza sauce for dipping. Serves 8 to 10.

Need to chill lots of bottles or cans of soda? You'll find they chill more quickly on ice than in the refrigerator. Just add beverages to an ice-filled cooler or galvanized tub...you'll save valuable space in the fridge too!

Pepperoni Squares

Green Chile Chicken Dip

## Green Chile Chicken Dip

*Easy to make and packed with zesty flavor...sure to become your next favorite dip!*

12-oz. can chicken, drained
2 8-oz. pkgs. cream cheese, softened and cubed
2 10-3/4 oz. cans cream of chicken soup

2 4-oz. cans diced green chiles
4-oz. can diced jalapeño peppers
tortilla chips

In a lightly greased 13"x9" baking pan, combine all ingredients except tortilla chips. Do not drain chiles or peppers. Stir until well blended. Bake, uncovered, at 350 degrees for 20 to 25 minutes, until hot and bubbly. Serve warm with tortilla chips. Serves 10 to 12.

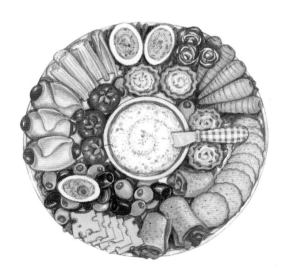

A casual appetizer party is perfect for catching up with family & friends. Everyone is sure to discover new favorites, so be sure to have each person bring along extra copies of their recipe to share.

## Country Caviar

*One of our favorite dips! It's easy to make and keeps for days in the fridge, if it lasts that long. Spice it to suit to your taste, from mild to extra hot.*

15-oz. can black, red or pinto
    beans, drained
11-oz. can sweet corn & diced
    peppers, drained
10-oz. can mild, medium or hot
    diced tomatoes with green
    chiles, drained

6 green onions, chopped
2 c. shredded Monterey Jack or
    Pepper Jack cheese
1 c. light mayonnaise
1 c. light sour cream
hot pepper sauce to taste
pita chips or tortilla chips

Mix together all ingredients except chips in a 13"x9" glass baking pan or serving bowl. Cover and chill; may be kept refrigerated for several days. Serve with warm pita chips or tortilla chips. Serves 8 to 10.

Kitchen shears are so handy for snipping fresh herbs, cutting stewed tomatoes right in the can and chopping green onions. Remember to wash them with soap and water after each use.

Country Caviar

Game-Time Party Mix

## Game-Time Party Mix

*Mix up a batch of this salty-sweet snack for guests to munch on...
they'll love it!*

2 c. bite-size crispy corn cereal
   squares
2 c. mini pretzels
1 c. peanuts

1 c. caramels, unwrapped and
   coarsely chopped
11-oz. pkg. butterscotch chips

Combine cereal, pretzels, peanuts and caramels in a large bowl. In a
microwave-safe bowl, microwave butterscotch chips on medium power for
one minute; stir. Microwave an additional 15 seconds and stir; repeat until
melted and smooth. Pour over cereal mixture; stir to coat evenly. Spread
mixture into a 13"x9" baking pan coated with non-stick vegetable spray.
Let stand 20 minutes, or until firm. Break into small pieces. Store in a
loosely covered container. Makes about 6 cups.

Start a family game night! Get out all your favorite board games and
play to your heart's content. Small prizes for winners and bowls of
snack mix or popcorn are a must!

## Spiced Orange Pecans

*Fill a pretty pail with these scrumptious nuts for a hostess gift that's sure to be welcome.*

2 egg whites, beaten
3 T. orange juice
2 c. pecan halves
1-1/2 c. powdered sugar
2 T. cornstarch

1 T. orange zest
1 t. cinnamon
3/4 t. ground cloves
1/4 t. allspice
1/8 t. salt

In a large bowl, whisk together egg whites and orange juice. Add pecans and toss to coat; drain. In a separate bowl, combine remaining ingredients; mix well. Add pecans and toss to coat. Spread pecans in a single layer in a greased 13"x9" baking pan. Bake, uncovered, at 250 degrees for 30 to 35 minutes, stirring occasionally, until dry and lightly golden. Cool completely; store in an airtight container. Makes about 3-1/2 cups.

Sweet or spicy candied nuts make a tasty, crunchy salad garnish...just coarsely chop and sprinkle on.

Spiced Orange Pecans

Munch & Crunch Mix

## Munch & Crunch Mix

*A crunchy snack mix with a kick of chili and cayenne! Tie little sacks of this spicy mix in bandannas for a game-day treat.*

1 c. mini pretzels
1 c. corn chips
1 c. oyster crackers
1 c. toasted pumpkin seeds
1 c. honey-roasted peanuts
2 T. butter, melted

2 T. brown sugar, packed
1 t. Worcestershire sauce
1 t. chili powder
1/2 t. onion salt
1/2 t. ground cumin
1/8 t. cayenne pepper

Combine pretzels, chips, crackers, seeds and nuts in a large bowl; toss to mix. Whisk together remaining ingredients; pour over mixture in bowl, stirring to coat. Spread mix in an ungreased 13"x9" baking pan. Bake, uncovered, at 300 degrees for 25 minutes, stirring after 12 minutes. Cool completely; store in an airtight container. Makes about 5 cups.

For fun party favors, fill clear plastic cups with crunchy snack mix. Seal with sheets of colorful plastic wrap to keep the goodies inside. Heap the cups in a basket...guests can choose a favorite to take home.

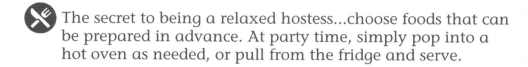

 The secret to being a relaxed hostess...choose foods that can be prepared in advance. At party time, simply pop into a hot oven as needed, or pull from the fridge and serve.

 Make it easy for guests to mingle and chat...set up food at several tables instead of one big party buffet. Place hot foods on one table, chilled foods at another, sweets and beverages at yet another.

 Try serving "light" dippers with full-flavored hot dips and spreads. Fresh veggies, pita wedges, baked tortilla chips and multi-grain crispbread are all sturdy enough to scoop up dips, yet won't overshadow the flavor of the dip.

 Glass or dark baking pans will retain more heat than shiny ones. Unless the recipe specifies a glass pan, be sure to reduce the oven temperature by 25 degrees when using them.

# Sweets
# to Share

# Sweets to Share

## Spiced Zucchini Bars

*You'll never exclaim, "too many zucchini!" again, once you've sampled these yummy bars.*

2 c. all-purpose flour
2 t. baking soda
1/2 t. salt
2 t. cinnamon
3 eggs, beaten
1 c. oil
2 c. sugar

1 t. vanilla extract
1 t. lemon juice
1 c. raisins
2 c. zucchini, grated
3/4 c. chopped nuts
16-oz. container cream cheese
   frosting

In a bowl, combine flour, baking soda, salt and cinnamon; set aside. In a separate bowl, whisk together eggs, oil, sugar, vanilla and lemon juice. Gradually add flour mixture to egg mixture. Fold in remaining ingredients except frosting; pour into a greased and floured 13"x9" baking pan. Bake at 325 degrees for 25 to 35 minutes, until lightly golden. Cool; spread with frosting. Cut into bars. Makes 3 dozen.

## Beth's Toffee Bars

*These scrumptious bars will disappear as fast as they hit the table... they're that good!*

18-1/2 oz. pkg. yellow cake mix
1 egg, beaten
1/3 c. butter, melted and slightly
   cooled

6-oz. pkg. toffee bits
14-oz. can sweetened condensed
   milk

In a large bowl, stir together dry cake mix, egg and butter. Gently pat into a 13"x9" baking pan. Sprinkle with toffee bits; spread condensed milk over the top. Bake at 350 degrees for about 25 minutes. Cool; cut into squares. Makes about 16 bars.

For perfect bar cookies and brownies, line the baking pan with aluminum foil, then grease the foil. Once the cookies have baked and cooled, lift them out onto a cutting board, where they can be neatly sliced.

Spiced Zucchini Bars

Ben's Pecan Blondies

## Ben's Pecan Blondies

*A very old-fashioned cookie bar...they're still delicious!*

1 c. sugar
1/2 c. brown sugar, packed
1/2 c. butter, softened
2 eggs, beaten
1 t. vanilla extract

1-1/2 c. all-purpose flour
1 t. baking powder
1/2 t. salt
1/2 c. chopped pecans
Garnish: pecan halves

In a large bowl, beat sugars and butter until fluffy. Blend in eggs and vanilla. Add flour, baking powder and salt; mix well. Stir in chopped pecans. Spread batter in a greased 13"x9" baking pan. Bake at 350 degrees for 25 to 35 minutes. Cool one hour; frost with Browned Butter Frosting. Cut into bars; garnish with pecan halves. Makes 3 dozen.

## Browned Butter Frosting:

2 T. butter
2 c. powdered sugar

1/4 t. vanilla extract
2 to 4 T. milk

Melt butter in a saucepan over medium heat until light golden brown. Remove from heat. Stir in powdered sugar, vanilla and enough milk for desired consistency.

Life is uncertain; eat dessert first!
-Ernestine Ulmer

## 4-Layer Cookie Bars

*A crunchy, creamy no-bake dessert everyone will enjoy.*

16-oz. pkg. rectangular buttery
  crackers, divided
1/2 c. butter
2/3 c. sugar
1/2 c. brown sugar, packed

1 c. graham cracker crumbs
1/4 c. milk
2/3 c. creamy peanut butter
1/2 c. semi-sweet chocolate chips
1/2 c. peanut butter chips

Line the bottom of a buttered 13"x9" baking pan with a single layer of crackers; set aside. Melt butter in a heavy saucepan over low heat; add sugars, graham cracker crumbs and milk. Cook over medium-high heat until sugars dissolve, stirring often; spread over crackers in pan. Arrange another single layer of crackers on top; set aside. Combine remaining ingredients in a separate saucepan; cook over low heat until melted, stirring until smooth and creamy. Spread over crackers; let stand until firm. Cut into bars. Makes 2 dozen.

## Mango Citrus Bars

*Just a little change to the traditional lemon bar recipe...wonderful!*

1 c. butter, melted
1/2 c. powdered sugar
2-1/4 c. all-purpose flour, divided
4 eggs, beaten

2 c. sugar
1/4 c. mango juice
1 t. lemon or lime zest
Garnish: powdered sugar

Combine melted butter, powdered sugar and 2 cups flour. Press into the bottom of a lightly greased 13"x9" baking pan. Bake at 350 degrees for 15 to 20 minutes. Mix together remaining flour, eggs, sugar, juice and zest; pour over baked crust. Return to oven and bake an additional 20 minutes. Dust with powdered sugar. Cool and cut into bars. Makes 20.

Cut bar cookies with a plastic knife for a clean cut every time.

4-Layer Cookie Bars

Chocolate-Raspberry Brownies

## Chocolate-Raspberry Brownies

*A layer of raspberry preserves makes these brownies really special!*

1 c. butter
5 1-oz. sqs. unsweetened baking
    chocolate, chopped
2 c. sugar
4 eggs, beaten
2 t. vanilla extract

1-1/4 c. all-purpose flour
1 t. baking powder
1/2 t. salt
1 c. chopped walnuts, toasted
1/2 c. raspberry preserves

Melt butter and chocolate in a heavy saucepan over low heat, stirring constantly, until smooth. Remove from heat. Whisk in sugar, eggs and vanilla; set aside. In a small bowl, mix flour, baking powder and salt. Add to chocolate mixture and whisk to blend; stir in nuts. Spread 2 cups batter in a greased 13"x9" baking pan. Freeze until firm, about 20 minutes. Spread preserves over frozen batter in pan; spoon remaining batter over preserves. Let stand 20 minutes to thaw. Bake at 350 degrees for about 35 minutes, until a toothpick tests clean. Cut into squares; transfer to a wire rack to cool. Makes 2 dozen.

A scrumptious solution for crumbly brownies! In stemmed glasses, alternate layers of ice cream and crumbled brownie. Garnish with whipped topping and a sprinkle of chopped nuts...no one will ever know the difference.

## Salted Nut Roll Bars

*Salty, sweet, crunchy and gooey...every bite satisfies!*

18-1/2 oz. pkg. yellow cake mix
1 egg, beaten
1/4 c. butter, melted and slightly
   cooled
3 c. mini marshmallows
10-oz. pkg. peanut butter chips

1/2 c. light corn syrup
1/2 c. butter, softened
1 t. vanilla extract
2 c. salted peanuts
2 c. crispy rice cereal

Combine dry cake mix, egg and melted butter; press into a greased 13"x9" baking pan. Bake at 350 degrees for 10 to 12 minutes. Sprinkle marshmallows over baked crust; return to oven and bake for 3 additional minutes, or until marshmallows are melted. In a saucepan over medium heat, melt peanut butter chips, corn syrup, butter and vanilla. Stir until smooth; stir in nuts and cereal. Spread mixture over marshmallow layer. Chill briefly until firm; cut into squares. Makes 2-1/2 dozen.

Vintage china plates can be picked up for a song at yard sales. They're just right for delivering cookies to a neighbor or your child's teacher... and there's no need for them to return the plate!

Salted Nut Roll Bars

Cinnamon Cream Cheese Squares

## Cinnamon Cream Cheese Squares

*Scrumptious warm or cold...a delicious breakfast treat or dinnertime dessert.*

2 8-oz. tubes refrigerated crescent rolls
8-oz. pkg. cream cheese, softened
1 t. vanilla extract

1/2 c. sugar
1/4 c. butter, melted
cinnamon-sugar to taste

Unroll one tube of crescent rolls and arrange in a lightly greased 13"x9" baking pan. Pinch seams together and set aside. In a bowl, beat together cream cheese, vanilla and sugar; spread over rolls in pan. Top with remaining tube of crescent rolls, pinching together seams. Drizzle melted butter over top; sprinkle with cinnamon-sugar. Bake at 350 degrees for 30 minutes, or until golden. cool; cut into squares. Makes 10 to 12 servings.

A no-mess method for greasing and flouring baking pans: Simply grease the pan, sprinkle generously with flour, cover with plastic wrap and shake!

## Quick Lunchbox Cake

*What kid wouldn't love to find a wrapped chunk of this yummy cake in his or her lunchbox? Moms will love that it's easy to handle and not messy.*

2-1/4 c. all-purpose flour
2 t. baking soda
1 t. salt
1 c. brown sugar, packed
2 eggs, beaten

1/4 c. butter, softened
1 c. fruit cocktail, drained
1/2 c. semi-sweet chocolate chips
1/2 c. chopped nuts

In a large bowl, combine all ingredients except chocolate chips and nuts. Beat well with an electric mixer on low speed until smooth. Pour batter into a greased and floured 13"x9" baking pan. Sprinkle chips and nuts over batter. Bake at 350 degrees for 35 to 40 minutes. Cool and cut into squares. Makes 16 servings.

## Fruit Cocktail Cake

*Great when you're busy and your budget is tight...it's super-fast and uses just a few ordinary ingredients!*

1-1/2 c. sugar
2 c. all-purpose flour
2 t. baking soda

2 eggs, beaten
15-oz. can fruit cocktail

In a large bowl, combine all ingredients except fruit cocktail; mix well. Add undrained fruit and stir well. Pour batter into a greased 13"x9" baking pan. Bake at 350 degrees for 30 to 40 minutes, until cake tests done with a toothpick inserted in center. Makes 12 servings.

When draining canned fruit, freeze the juice in ice cube trays...handy for adding a little sweetness to marinades and dressings.

Quick Lunchbox Cake

Tres Leches Cake

## Tres Leches Cake

*This yummy Mexican-inspired cake is sure to become a favorite! Its name means "cake of three milks." The fruit topping looks so pretty, it's worth taking the time to do it.*

18-1/4 oz. pkg. yellow cake mix
14-oz. can sweetened condensed
   milk
5-oz. can evaporated milk
7.6-oz. can media crema, or
   1 c. whole milk

8-oz. container frozen whipped
   topping, thawed
Optional: sliced strawberries, kiwi,
   pineapple, mandarin oranges

Prepare cake mix according to package instructions; bake in a greased 13"x9" baking pan. While cake is still warm, pierce surface every 1/2 inch with a skewer. Combine milks in a bowl; pour slowly and evenly over cake. Let cake stand at room temperature for 30 minutes. Cover with plastic wrap; refrigerate for at least 30 minutes, or until well chilled. At serving time, frost cake with whipped topping; decorate with fruit, if desired. Keep refrigerated. Serves 8 to 10.

Evaporated milk and sweetened condensed milk are handy, but not not interchangeable in recipes. Condensed milk contains sugar and is cooked down to a thickened consistency, while evaporated milk contains no added sugar.

## Almond Amaretto Bread Pudding

*So simple to make, yet looks and tastes so special!*

1 qt. half-and-half
1 loaf Italian bread, cubed
3 eggs
1-1/2 c. sugar

2 T. almond extract
1 c. golden raisins
3/4 c. sliced almonds

In a large bowl, pour half-and-half over bread and stir gently. Cover and refrigerate 30 minutes to one hour. In a separate bowl, beat eggs until they begin to foam. Add sugar; mix well. Stir in almond extract, raisins and almonds. Add to bread mixture and mix well. Pour into a lightly greased 13"x9" baking pan. Bake at 325 degrees for 50 minutes. Serve warm with Amaretto Sauce. Serves 12.

### Amaretto Sauce:

1/2 c. butter
1 c. powdered sugar
1 egg, beaten

1/4 c. amaretto liqueur, or 1 T.
    almond extract plus 3 T. water

Melt butter in a double boiler. Beat in remaining ingredients. Cook, stirring constantly, until mixture begins to thicken.

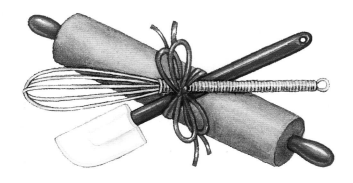

Almond Amaretto Bread Pudding

Strawberry-Nectarine Cobbler

# Sweets to Share

## Strawberry-Nectarine Cobbler

*Make this refreshing cobbler with summer-ripe fruit...yum! Add a scoop of ice cream, if you like.*

6 to 8 nectarines, pitted and very
    thinly sliced
1/4 c. light brown sugar, packed
1 t. cinnamon
1/4 t. nutmeg
1 t. salt
2 c. fresh strawberries, hulled
    and halved

2 T. butter, sliced
1/2 c. sugar, divided
1 egg, beaten
1 T. baking powder
1 c. all-purpose flour
1 T. vanilla extract
1/2 c. milk

Combine nectarines, brown sugar, spices and salt in a bowl; let stand for 15 minutes. In a saucepan over low heat, combine strawberries, butter and 1/4 cup sugar. Cook and stir for 5 minutes, until syrupy. Remove from heat; cool. In another bowl, whisk together egg, remaining sugar, baking powder, flour, vanilla and milk. Spread nectarine mixture evenly in an ungreased 13"x9" glass baking pan. Spoon strawberry mixture evenly over nectarines. Dollop with spoonfuls of batter. Bake at 350 degrees for 30 to 35 minutes. Cool at least 15 minutes before serving. Serves 12.

## Chocolate-Covered Cherry Cake

*Need a potluck dessert in a hurry? This is so delicious, and no one will believe how easy it is to make!*

2 21-oz. cans cherry pie filling
18-1/2 oz. pkg. chocolate cake mix
1 c. butter, sliced

2-1/4 oz. pkg. chopped pecans
2 T. sugar
Garnish: vanilla ice cream

Add pie filling to a lightly greased 13"x9" baking pan. Sprinkle dry cake mix evenly over pie filling. Distribute butter slices evenly over cake mix. Sprinkle evenly with pecans and sugar. Bake at 350 degrees for 35 to 45 minutes. Serve warm, topped with scoops of ice cream. Makes 8 to 10 servings.

## Pineapple-Cherry Crisp

*Quick & easy to make, and most of the ingredients can be kept in the pantry for a spur-of-the-moment treat. Can't beat that!*

20-oz. can crushed pineapple, well
   drained
2 21-oz. cans cherry pie filling
18-1/2 oz. pkg. white cake mix

1/2 c. butter, thinly sliced
3/4 c. chopped pecans
Garnish: whipped cream or ice
   cream

Spread pineapple evenly in an ungreased 13"x9" baking pan. Spoon pie filling over pineapple. Sprinkle dry cake mix on top; dot with butter and top with pecans. Bake at 350 degrees for 45 minutes, or until bubbly and topping is golden. Serve warm or cooled, garnished as desired. Makes 12 to 15 servings.

Share your best berry dessert! Fill a plastic zipping bag with the dry ingredients; seal. Wrap the bag in a square of checked fabric and tie closed with ribbon. Give with a recipe card and a pint of fresh berries from the farmers' market.

Pineapple-Cherry Crisp

Grandma Gracie's Lemon Cake

# Sweets to Share

## Grandma Gracie's Lemon Cake

*You will simply love this lemony cake for any special occasion!*

18-1/4 oz. pkg. yellow cake mix
3.4-oz. pkg. instant lemon pudding
  mix
3/4 c. oil

3/4 c. water
4 eggs, beaten
Garnish: powdered sugar

Combine all ingredients except garnish in a bowl; beat until well mixed. Pour batter into a greased 13"x9" baking pan. Bake at 350 degrees for 35 to 40 minutes, until a toothpick inserted in center comes out clean. Immediately poke holes through cake with a fork; pour glaze over cake. Dust with powdered sugar. Serves 10 to 12.

### Glaze:

2 c. powdered sugar
2 T. butter, melted

2 T. water
1/3 c. lemon juice

Combine all ingredients; stir until smooth.

## Strawberry Festival Cake

*A luscious dessert that's easy to make. You can't beat that!*

2 c. all-purpose flour
1 c. butter, melted
1 c. chopped nuts
1 c. plus 2 T. powdered sugar,
  divided

8-oz. pkg. cream cheese, softened
1 c. frozen whipped topping,
  thawed
4 c. strawberries, hulled and sliced
1 c. whipping cream

Mix together flour, butter and nuts. Press into a greased 13"x9" baking pan. Bake at 350 degrees for 25 minutes; cool. In a separate bowl, blend together one cup powdered sugar and cream cheese; fold in whipped topping. Spread over baked layer; cover and refrigerate until set. Arrange strawberries on top, reserving a small amount for garnish. Beat cream with an electric mixer on high speed until soft peaks form; gradually beat in remaining powdered sugar. Spread whipped cream over top. Garnish with reserved strawberries. Cover and refrigerate until serving time. Serves 12.

## Strawberry Dessert

*With only five ingredients, this dessert is simply almost too good to be true!*

16-1/2 oz. tube refrigerated sugar cookie dough
8-oz. pkg. cream cheese, softened
8-oz. container frozen whipped topping, thawed and divided
1 qt. strawberries, hulled and sliced
13-1/2 oz. container strawberry glaze

Slice cookie dough; press into the bottom of an ungreased 13"x9" baking pan. Bake at 350 degrees for 13 to 16 minutes, until lightly golden. Cool completely on a wire rack. Mix cream cheese and one cup whipped topping. Spread over cookie crust. Stir strawberries and glaze together and spread over top. Cover and chill. Cut into squares and serve with remaining whipped topping. Serves 10 to 12.

Use a plastic drinking straw to hull strawberries with ease. Just push the straw through the end without a stem and the green, leafy top will pop right off!

Strawberry Dessert

Isabella's Ice Cream Pie

## Isabella's Ice Cream Pie

*Make this yummy frozen dessert for your next picnic or cookout...
it feeds a crowd!*

2 c. bite-size crispy rice cereal
  squares, crushed
1 c. brown sugar, packed
1/2 c. sweetened flaked coconut
1/2 c. chopped almonds

1/2 c. butter, softened
1/2 gal. vanilla ice cream, softened
1 pt. orange, raspberry or lime
  sherbet, softened
Optional: candy sprinkles

In a large bowl, combine cereal, brown sugar, coconut, almonds and butter. Blend well; press mixture into an ungreased 13"x9" baking pan. Cover and chill well. Spread ice cream in crust; top with sherbet. Cover and freeze until set. Let stand at room temperature about 15 minutes before serving time. Cut into squares. Garnish with sprinkles, if desired. Serves 12 to 15.

## Turtle Pie

*A quick & easy favorite for any occasion.*

1/2 c. brown sugar, packed
1 c. all-purpose flour
3/4 c. chopped nuts
1/2 c. butter, melted

14-oz. jar caramel topping, divided
2 qts. vanilla ice cream, slightly
  softened

In a bowl, mix together sugar, flour, nuts and butter. Spread mixture on a lightly greased baking sheet; bake at 400 degrees for 10 minutes, or until crisp. Cool completely. Crumble crust and transfer to a 13"x9" baking pan, reserving 1/4 cup for topping. Pour half the jar of caramel over crumbled crust. Spread ice cream over caramel. Drizzle with remaining caramel; sprinkle with reserved crust crumbles. Cover and freeze for at least 2 hours before serving. Cut into squares. Serves 24.

For toasty flavor and color, simply spread shredded coconut on an ungreased baking sheet and bake for 5 to 7 minutes at 350 degrees.

## Frosty Butter Pecan Crunch Pie

*Chocolate and toffee come together sweetly in this scrumptious frozen pie.*

2 c. graham cracker crumbs
1/2 c. butter, melted
2 3.4-oz. pkgs. instant vanilla
   pudding mix
2 c. milk
1 qt. butter pecan ice cream,
   slightly softened

8-oz. container frozen whipped
   topping, thawed
2 chocolate-covered toffee candy
   bars, crushed

Combine graham cracker crumbs and melted butter in a bowl; pat mixture into an ungreased 13"x9" baking pan. Freeze until firm. In a large bowl, combine dry pudding mix and milk. Beat with an electric mixer on medium speed for about one minute, until well blended. Fold in ice cream and whipped topping; spoon over chilled crust. Sprinkle with candy bar pieces; cover and freeze until firm. Remove from freezer 20 minutes before serving. Serves 12 to 15.

Quickly soften ice cream in the carton using the microwave on high setting. For one pint, heat for 10 to 15 seconds; one quart, 15 to 25 seconds and 1/2 gallon, 30 to 40 seconds.

Frosty Butter Pecan Crunch Pie

Nathaniel's Chocolate Bowl

## Nathaniel's Chocolate Bowl

*Any day is a special occasion to fix what your family loves!*

15-1/4 oz. pkg. devil's food
  cake mix
1 c. water
1/2 c. oil
3 eggs, beaten
2 3.4-oz. pkgs. instant chocolate
  pudding mix

4 c. milk
16-oz. container frozen whipped
  topping, thawed
1 c. mini semi-sweet chocolate
  chips

Prepare cake mix with water, oil and eggs according to package directions; bake in a greased 13"x9" baking pan. Cool completely; cut into one-inch cubes. Meanwhile, prepare pudding mixes with milk according to package directions. In a large glass trifle bowl, layer half each of cake cubes, pudding and whipped topping. Repeat layers, ending with topping. Sprinkle with chocolate chips. Cover and chill until serving time. Serves 10 to 12.

Freeze dollops of whipped cream ahead of time...what a time-saver! Drop heaping tablespoonfuls onto a chilled baking sheet and freeze. Remove from the baking sheet and store in a plastic zipping bag. At serving time, place a dollop on a dessert portion...it will thaw quickly.

## Cream Cheese Crescent Bars

*Taking these bars to a carry-in dinner? Bring along some copies of the recipe...you're sure to get requests!*

2 8-oz. tubes refrigerated crescent rolls, separated
2 8-oz. pkgs. cream cheese, softened
1 t. vanilla extract
2/3 c. sugar
1 egg, separated

Line the bottom of a greased 13"x9" baking pan with one package crescent rolls, pinching seams together; set aside. Blend together cream cheese, vanilla, sugar and egg yolk; spread evenly over crust. Gently place remaining crescent roll dough on top, pinching together seams. In a bowl, whisk egg white until frothy; brush over dough. Sprinkle with Cinnamon Topping; bake at 350 degrees until golden, about 25 to 30 minutes. Cool; slice into bars or triangles. Makes 2 dozen.

### Cinnamon Topping:

1/2 c. sugar
1/4 c. chopped pecans
1 t. cinnamon

Gently mix together all ingredients.

Give bar cookies a fresh new look! Instead of bars or squares, cut cookies into diamond shapes.

Cream Cheese Crescent Bars

Everyone loves a dessert pizza! Press ready-made sugar cookie dough into an ungreased 13"x9" baking pan and bake as directed. Let crust cool, then spread with a mixture of one 8-ounce package cream cheese, one cup sugar and one teaspoon vanilla. Top with fresh fruit and cut into wedges.

Grandma always said, "Never return a dish empty." Gather up baking pans, cookie tins and pie plates that have been left behind, fill them with homebaked goodies and return them to their owners...they'll be pleasantly surprised!

To avoid scratching non-stick baking pans, be sure to serve up desserts using plastic or wood spatulas, never metal.

Short on time? Spread cookie dough in a 13"x9" baking pan and make bar cookies instead of individual drop cookies... they'll be just as delicious!

# Index

# Index

# Index

all-American * just like Mom's *hearty*

old-fashioned

satisfying

laughter

homestyle

homecooked *Good food* homecooked *tried & true*

# U.S. to Metric Recipe Equivalents

## Volume Measurements

| | |
|---|---|
| 1/4 teaspoon | 1 mL |
| 1/2 teaspoon | 2 mL |
| 1 teaspoon | 5 mL |
| 1 tablespoon = 3 teaspoons | 15 mL |
| 2 tablespoons = 1 fluid ounce | 30 mL |
| 1/4 cup | 60 mL |
| 1/3 cup | 75 mL |
| 1/2 cup = 4 fluid ounces | 125 mL |
| 1 cup = 8 fluid ounces | 250 mL |
| 2 cups = 1 pint =16 fluid ounces | 500 mL |
| 4 cups = 1 quart | 1 L |

## Weights

| | |
|---|---|
| 1 ounce | 30 g |
| 4 ounces | 120 g |
| 8 ounces | 225 g |
| 16 ounces = 1 pound | 450 g |

## Oven Temperatures

| | |
|---|---|
| 300° F | 150° C |
| 325° F | 160° C |
| 350° F | 180° C |
| 375° F | 190° C |
| 400° F | 200° C |
| 450° F | 230° C |

## Baking Pan Sizes

*Square*

| | |
|---|---|
| 8x8x2 inches | 2 L = 20x20x5 cm |
| 9x9x2 inches | 2.5 L = 23x23x5 cm |

*Rectangular*

| | |
|---|---|
| 13x9x2 inches | 3.5 L = 33x23x5 cm |

*Loaf*

| | |
|---|---|
| 9x5x3 inches | 2 L = 23x13x7 cm |

*Round*

| | |
|---|---|
| 8x1-1/2 inches | 1.2 L = 20x4 cm |
| 9x1-1/2 inches | 1.5 L = 23x4 cm |